community 2.0

AT THE INTERSECTION OF DIGITAL MEDIA AND INFORMATION DESIGN

JOHN A. MCARTHUR, EDITOR

Copyright © 2012   John A. McArthur

All rights reserved.

Cover art and formatting by J.A. McArthur
www.jamcarthur.com

ISBN:147507851X
ISBN-13: 978-1475078510

Table of Contents

Introduction   1
    John A. McArthur

Designing Consumer Communities: 5
The demand for online customer service
    Kristen Bostedo-Conway

Voicing a Campus Icon: 25
Twitter, a bronze goddess, and
hyperlocal community engagement
    John A. McArthur

Finding Community through Blogging   45
    Jennifer L. Hull

Growing with the Millennial Generation: 61
Designing digital media for college student recruitment
    Emily Carrara

Designing Online Credibility: 81
Bloggers as leaders in audience and expertise
    Kenyon Stanley

QR Codes: Click, snap, save to erase the digital divide   97
    Davida Jackson

Investing in Digital Senior Citizens   109
    Sandra Saburn

Editor's Note   121

Introduction

John A. McArthur, Editor

Community 2.0 began as an effort to explore the impacts of digital media technology and information design on communities, broadly defined. Each chapter in the book defines community differently. In one chapter, the community is the network of social support created by a health care blog. In another, the community is geographic. Others define communities as groups of people with shared interests. Yet another examines communities created by lack of access to technology. But whether created by circumstance, geography, or interest, these communities are representative of the types of communities whose presence are expanding as digital technology reshapes our ability to connect with people.

Each chapter combines at least one digital media technology and several information design principles as they apply to the creation or development of the author's chosen community. The digital media covered in this text are diverse, but most are reflective of current trends in participatory media. Facebook, Twitter, blogs, interactive websites, and other Web 2.0 technologies are all discussed in relation to particular communities and in the context of specific goals.

By applying information design principles to the topics addressed, each chapter studies these digital media forms to better understand how a community might use a technology to connect people to people. Information design, for the purposes of this book, might best be defined as "the systematic arrangement and use of communication carriers, channels, and [symbols] to increase the conversation of those participating in a specific conversation or discourse" (Jacobson, 1999, p.4). In other words, information design is first the construction and delivery of communication messages for maximum impact. Jacobson's addendum to this definition compels us to consider people and their communities.

The information design principles discussed are pulled from the fields of product design, technical communication, user-experience design, psychology, communication, and behavioral studies, just to name a few (see Albers & Mazur, 2003, for a summary of this area of study). Yet each chapter shares the goal of applying information design to the digital technologies discussed, toward the development of a particular community.

Overview of Contents

In the first chapter, marketing executive Kristen Bostedo-Conway explores communities created by organizations for customers. She targets the relationship between organizations and their customer communities to investigate how engaging customers in an experience might shift the way that companies approach traditional customer service. Using case studies from Nestle, Pottery Barn, and Best Buy, Bostedo-Conway explores the role that digital media can play and discusses strategies for effective design of customer service experiences.

In *Voicing a Campus Icon*, professor and researcher John A. McArthur examines a tweeting statue to ascertain how such objects can contribute to the development of hyperlocal communities around these objects. Based in information and product design, the chapter gives tangible examples of the types of visceral, cognitive, and affective responses arising from the statue's tweets as demonstrated through one community's use of social media.

Jennifer L. Hull turns our attention to the blogging community, specifically health care blogs, to investigate how a good combination of digital media technology and information design can create a seamless experience for authors and readers. Using the example of caringbridge.org, Hull examines the social support that blogging communities can provide and devotes attention to the medium itself. The chapter discusses the difference between designing a blog and developing a community.

Emily Carrara delves into the world of collegiate recruiting. In her examination of contemporary digital tools used in recruiting, Carrara claims that the traditional glossy mailer is now sharing time with the Facebook fan page for a community of students in the millennial generation. The chapter investigates (1) the university webpage and (2) the university Facebook page and their respective roles in college student recruitment.

How does a blogger develop credibility and expertise online ? Kenyon Stanley's chapter explores the mystique of digital credibility. His answer to that question is a combination of information design, digital media expertise, and research into the role of credibility in online environments. That credibility, he argues, is the thing that allows an individual blogger to become a leader in a community of interest.

Davida Jackson takes on the issues surrounding the digital divide and access to technology among lower socio-economic communities. She positions mobile optimization and the QR (quick response) code as components of a trajectory that could narrow the gap. She applies information design as she considers not only the delivery of a message, but also the technology a user employs to retrieve that message.

Finally, Sandy Saburn investigates senior citizens, advocating that information design can address issues of product design and user confidence in this growing population. The digital divide issues in relation to age can inspire us to create communities of education and training in digital literacy.

Digital and Media Literacy

All of these chapters are situated in a growing discussion in the merging fields of digital and media literacy. In *Digital & Media Literacy: A Plan of Action*, Renee Hobbs defines digital and media literacy as:

> A constellation of life skills that are necessary for full participation in our media-saturated, information-rich society. They include the ability to do the following:
>
> - Make responsible choices and access information by locating and sharing materials and comprehending information and ideas.
> - Analyze messages in a variety of forms by identifying the author, purpose and point of view, and evaluating the quality and credibility of the content.

- Create content in a variety of forms, making use of language, images, sound, and new digital tools and technologies.
- Reflect on one's own conduct and communication behavior by applying social responsibility and ethical principles.
- Take social action by working individually and collaboratively to share knowledge and solve problems in the family, workplace and community, and by participating as a member of a community. (Hobbs, 2010, p. vii-viii)

These abilities to access, analyze, create, reflect, and act remain fundamental to our society. They combine the ability to use technology with the ability to engage in civic discourse on the issues raised by technology.

This book is at once a reflection on our own use of technology and an action, as we attempt to offer our collective knowledge into this growing conversation. Furthermore, this discussion recognizes the fundamental role and responsibility we all share – to engage with and contribute to our communities.

As our society becomes more saturated with digital technologies, members in and leaders of every type of community will be challenged to incorporate, assess, and even design digital media tools and experiences for their communities. This book aims to integrate information design squarely into that discussion as a tool and framework for building experiences that can create and shape the communities we serve.

References

Albers, M., & Mazur, B. (Eds.) (2003). *Content and Complexity: Information design in technical communication.* Mahwah, NJ: Lawrence Erlbaum & Associates, Inc.

Hobbs, R. (2010). *Digital & Media Literacy: A plan of action.* Washington, DC: The Aspen Institute.

Jacobson, R. (1999). *Information Design.* Cambridge, Mass.: MIT Press.

Designing Consumer Communities:
The demand for online customer service

Kristen Bostedo-Conway

Computer mediated communication (CMC) is redefining the way organizations and consumers converse. In particular, social networking sites are increasing consumers' ability to engage and build relationships with organizations. In a 2010 research study entitled *The Impact of Online Brand Community Type on Consumer's Community Engagement Behaviors*, researchers state that altruism and social identification are strong motivations for consumers to engage in online brand community behaviors (Lee, Lee & Kim). Additionally, a 2011 research study published in *Social Behavior and Personality* stated that service marketers are increasingly trying to develop better customer service strategies. "Internet marketing is one of the increasingly important electronic marketing tools for enhancing customer attraction, delivering services, and executing transactions" (Luo & Lee, 2011, p. 825-826). The increase in CMC is fundamentally changing the way consumers and organizations communicate, suggesting a shift from linear to dyadic communication models.

For electronic marketing tools to support a dyadic communication model they have to be designed in a way that is both functional and informative. In *Experience Design 1.1*, Nathan Shedroff (2002) discusses the spectrum for understanding information. He believes that "information is really data transformed into something more valuable by building context around it so that it becomes more understandable" (p. 34). What Shedroff aptly describes is the ability of communication professionals to coalesce data into viable information. This information can be used to create knowledge and ultimately wisdom within communities.

Using Shedroff's model of information design, data turned into information turned into wisdom, this chapter will explore how social networking sites are impacting organizations' customer service models by reviewing four fundamental ideas shaping this linear to dyadic communication shift:

- Consumers' desire for two way communication with organizations
- The ability of organizations to create and cultivate online communities
- The impact of information design on customer engagement
- The significance of trust and dialogue in online and offline interactions

Grounding the ideas of creation, cultivation, information design and trust in research, an outline of fundamental practices will be developed enabling organizations to better interact with current and potential customers online.

Designing Customer Service Dialogue

Consumers' Desire for Two-Way Communication

Prior to CMC, communication between organizations and consumers occurred in a linear communication pattern. Organizations functioned as senders and consumers functioned as receivers. Over the years, however, the make-up of the United States economy has changed. In 2011 the service sector accounted for 70% of the United States economy (Jarvis, 2011). Due to the change in America's economy from goods to service, it is easy to infer that customer service also increased in importance forcing more industries to use it as primary differentiator. Therefore, ease of use, trust and satisfaction are becoming greater determinations of customer loyalty and purchase intent (Luo & Lee, 2011; Bolkan & Daly, 2009; Andrews, 2002).

Luo & Lee (2011) propose that resolving real-time related problems could lead to an increase in consumer trust and loyalty specifically for e-service marketing. Their study highlights the importance of real time resolution and connects it to the ability of an organization to grow. United

States consumers have a variety of purchase options available requiring companies to create innovative customer service solutions proving they deserve to be vendors of choice.

In exploring how organizations respond to customer complaints, Bolkan and Daily (2009) found that, when consumers take the time to voice a complaint, it is essential that the organization respond. Additionally, the company needs to be cognizant of how it responds communicating both "understanding and respect" (p. 37).

Communicating with customers in a way that is mutually beneficial can be seen as a new concept. In *The End of Business As Usual*, Solis (2012) describes how companies are achieving customer centricity in a development model that moves organizations from rigid information hoarders to adaptive, agile businesses easily functioning in a continually evolving ecosystem. The crux of this change is an organization's ability to move beyond social interaction. An organization might do this by truly connecting internal areas of the company with multiple external ecosystems, resulting in mutual gain (Solis, 2012). From the research one might deduce that the only way businesses will continue to thrive is if they listen and respond to customers' suggestions and requests. It truly is a 'Consumer Revolution' (Solis, 2012).

In a post on BrianSolis.com, one of the world's leading marketing and business strategy blogs, Frank Eliason describes why companies are failing and how change is inevitable if organizations are going to connect with customers:

> In my view disconnected businesses are attempting to placate consumers (through social media), to minimize or eliminate the complaint. For social media service to scale (throughout the organization), change *must* happen. Companies must care. The true transformation in a company comes from wholesale change. This involves building the back end to start fixing the problems that created negative experiences in the first place. *(Eliason, 2011)*

The change Eliason describes is the change from linear communication to dyadic. He concludes, correctly, that some companies are not truly changing their communication models. Instead they are simply being present in social media forums like Facebook and Twitter. Organizations will have to become open about processes and procedures before they can truly listen to consumers.

Both Solis and Eliason directly reference the shift that technology has created in consumer communication. Consumers demand dialogue. When Dell recently asked its customers if they would like to be able to connect with the company and its sales team via Google+ "hangouts" Dell received over 800 responses; most of them positive (Eliason, 2011). Dell's testing of Google+ is an example of how one company is trying to respond to consumers' demands. Dell, like other organizations, is beginning to understand that a one-way, linear communication model is insufficient. The increasing use of technology, specifically social media, has forced organizations to address consumers in a new way. No longer are they able to erect barriers inhibiting two-way communication. The open forum that technology has created means that control of communication has altered. Now, both consumers and organizations are senders and receivers of messages. As the use of mobile technology continues to increase, more and more organizations will be forced to listen, respond and even change based on their customers' feedback.

Creating and Cultivating Online Communities

As organizations search for ways to connect with stakeholders online, they must understand that connection is just the first step. To have meaningful stakeholder interaction organizations have to also nurture their online communities. Therefore, the question arises: Why would an individual want to connect with an organization online? The answer might be found in Henri Tajfel and John Turner's Social Identity Theory. Their concept of social identity is defined as an individual's self-concept being validated by membership in a particular social group (Tajfel & Turner, 1986). Similar to the construction of brand identities, online groups develop a following based on the perceived status of the group. This status supports the group's legitimacy. In turn both status and legitimacy affirm the user's desired social identity. This affirmation becomes the primary reason that individuals seek connection.

In a 2009 study on brand communities and engagement Lee, Kim, & Kim propose that social identification motivations are the primary reason for engagement. However, they note the importance for fostering a platform where consumers can share and exchange ideas versus imposing an organization's ideas on consumers. This observation suggests that interaction by members in online communities must occur in order to achieve ongoing cultivation.

Jin, Lee and Cheung (2011) focus on the ongoing cultivation of online communities in their study on predicting continued use. The study suggests that when people receive both informational and functional value from an online community they were more emotionally attached to the online group. Informational value is defined as information perceived to be high in quality and interesting to the consumer. Functional value references the ability of consumers to use and access the information easily. If an online group provides highly valuable information, but that information is difficult to access users will have less attachment to the online group. The inverse is also true. If an online group is organized extremely well, but does not provide valuable information consumers may disregard the site. Furthermore, online groups should be used with the understanding that the key purpose for the consumer is to access, share and discuss information.

As CMC continues to grow, understanding how online communities are formed and sustained will become more important. The best way to create and cultivate online communities is for organizations to identify with their stakeholders by providing a platform for information sharing that is:

- Functional – making information easily accessible by creating easy to use and well organized online tools and websites
- Useful – providing information perceived by stakeholders as highly valuable
- Interactive – creating the ability for stakeholders to engage with each other through the act of sharing. This involves consumers being able to share their own ideas in addition to sharing information the organization provides.

If organizations can achieve these three fundamentals, while consistently sharing new information, one can presume that they will be able to build rich, self-sustaining online communities.

Information Design & the Impact on Consumer Engagement

One of the key criteria for cultivating online communities is the functional ability of the online tool to share information effectively and efficiently. For guidance in developing these functional abilities, this chapter turns to information design.

In *A Three Part Framework for Information Design*, Carliner (2000) expresses how technical communicators are experiencing the move from developing ways to produce content to actually understanding how to develop content more effectively. Carliner describes how information design has emerged from the field of technical writing to become more like the instructional design of education courses and software engineering. This movement occurs as content creators are being asked to analyze, design, develop, implement and evaluate their messages. To say it more succinctly, information design is the ability to "present the right information to the right people at the right time, in the most effective and efficient form" (Horn, 1999, p.8).

In addition to the traditional definition of information design, Carliner (2000) suggests that information design goes beyond the simple exercise of effectively coalescing data and proposes a three level approach: physical (ability to find information), cognitive (ability to understand the information) and affective (the ability to be comfortable with the presentation of the information).

In *User Experience Design for Technical Communication: Expanding Our Notions of Quality Information Design*, Williams develops the idea of adding emotional response to information design by including user experience design as a criteria for designing quality information. Experience design recognizes the need to "consider people's thoughts and feelings, that is the interaction between cognition and affection" when designing information (Shriver, 2001, p. 8). As consumers demand two-way communication and begin to group themselves into online communities created by organizations and businesses it is plausible to conclude that the need to design information physically, cognitively and affectively intensifies.

In Experience Design 1.1, Nathan Shedroff explains information design as a continuum:

> One of the first things we learn about understanding is that it is a continuum from Data, a somewhat raw ingredient, to Wisdom, an ultimate achievement. Along this spectrum is an ever-increasing value chain of understanding which is derived from an increasing level of context and meaning that becomes more personal, more

sophisticated – not to mention more valuable – as it approaches Wisdom. (2002, p. 35)

[Data → Information → Knowledge → Wisdom]

A representation of Shedroff's (2002) continuum

Shedroff's definition captures the essence of information design in the Internet age. He skillfully describes the consumer's desire for valuable, personal interaction that achieves a greater understanding of the world. To create successful online communities, marketing and communication professionals must be able to coalesce data into accessible information that provides knowledge to the user, can be discussed amongst the group, and ultimately translates into wisdom for the community.

Further underscoring how important design is, Luo & Lee specifically found that trust and loyalty to an online community was created based upon the design of web pages (2011). Their findings are based on a 45-question 5-point Likert survey of 715 individuals that used international online travel agencies. The perception of trust and loyalty to a site positively increased when users believed the site was efficient, useful, and the information was readily available (Luo & Lee, 2011). In conclusion, Lou & Lee state: "In terms of upgrading e-service quality consumer's perception of value and customer service satisfaction e-service agencies should pay more attention to developing and improving the design of their websites" (p. 834). Their findings are a radical departure from the early days of text-based web design. This highlights the increasing importance design plays in the ability to use and understand data.

Pottery Barn provides a real world example of how designing information in a relevant and useful fashion for its customers can increase service. Using YouTube as the platform, the company created how-to videos about party planning and interior design to help customers learn more about Pottery Barn products. This proactive form of customer service helped earn them a Mashable Best Social Media Customer Service award in 2010 (Peters, 2010).

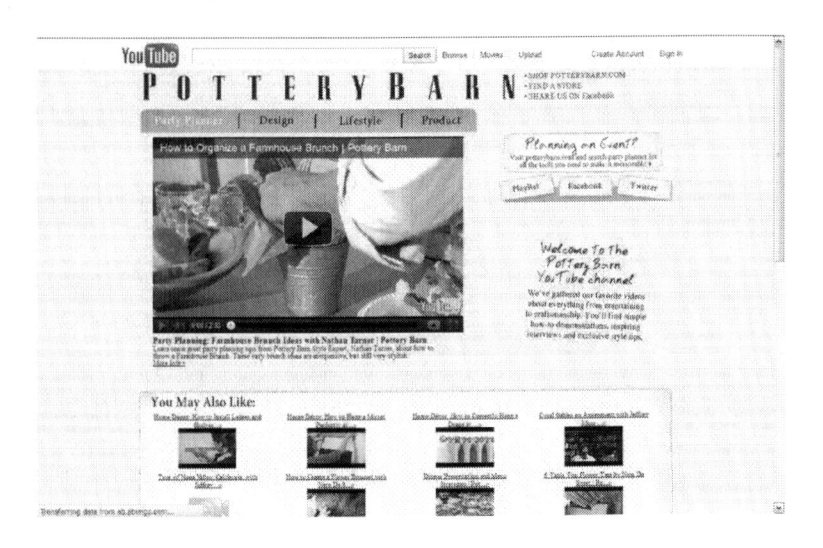

Screenshot of Pottery Barn's YouTube page

The videos are created to engage the customer. A section called 'You May Also Like' entices readers to peruse video catalogs instead of making them search or hunt for additional how-to ideas. Using YouTube was a strategic move on Pottery Barn's part for two main reasons:

1. YouTube is an existing platform that consumers already use to view videos. Designing a strategy on top of an existing platform helped Pottery Barn create and cultivate their community.
2. Consumers are already familiar with the functionality of YouTube making it easier to use over a new, unfamiliar platform.

Following Shedroff's model, Pottery Barn took data (products) and provided information about them via video – to create knowledge for customers. Since the videos showcase other products as well, customers reflect on new purchases. Ultimately the videos create wisdom as customers search the videos, reviewing how to best use Pottery Barn's products in their homes.

The usefulness of design is becoming more essential in the digital world and it is not a matter to be overlooked. As communication professionals develop online communities and customer service models the design of these sites must be tested and reviewed to ensure the data housed within them is easily accessible, informative and interactive.

The Significance of Trust

To understand how trust impacts customer service, this discussion will use Moran & Hunt's (1994) definition: Trust is the perception of confidence in an organizations reliability and integrity. As our world becomes more open, or public, through the use of social media tools the need for trust and the fears surrounding privacy grow. Jeff Jarvis (2011), author of *Public Parts*, believes that people have six main fears regarding their privacy in online communities. Jarvis' (2011) six fears restated are:

- Identity theft, which can ultimately lead to loss of money, financial stability and extreme stress.
- Unauthorized use of one's image or information for commercial gain.
- Manipulating information to defame character.
- Government control, surveillance, prosecution and persecution.
- Information flow, or the ability of computers to put together scattered bits of information so that our identities are available for everyone to see in all contexts: social, healthcare, financial, family, and work.
- Organizations' ability to bother us or "creep us out" with their knowledge about our activities and interests.

Jarvis' description of consumers' fear is founded. In 2011 the Play Station Network, run by Sony, had a breach compromising over 70 million records (Molina, 2011). Each record contained full names, email addresses, purchase history and credit card information. According to Molina, this network breach was the second largest ever . In a community used by so many, privacy and trust were completely obliterated creating a massive crisis and a major need for customer service recovery.

Luo & Lee's study titled *Influence of Trust and Usefulness on Customer Perceptions of E-Service Quality* shows that when trust and usefulness were both rated highly, the number of airline tickets purchased from an e-traveling service increased. Luo & Lee's study further illustrates that increased use was directly achieved when consumers trust the website from which they are purchasing.

Niklas Luhmann theorized about how communication could achieve trust when he developed his Theory of Communication Cycles. In the most basic form, Luhmann noted that communication was a closed, self-referential, social system that constantly repeats its own pattern (Luhmann, 2000b). Luhmann's two main ideas were reflection and reflexivity.

Luhmann defined reflexivity as the narcissistic perspective occurring within an organization and the organizations belief that their worldview is the only truth (Luhmann, 2000b). Reflection, on the other hand, occurs when an organization views itself from the outside and orients itself based on its environment.

According to Luhmann, when the organization uses one view and consumers use another dissonance is created within the communication cycle. Dissonance, defined as two parties lacking agreement, ultimately creates distrust. This distrust further illustrates the need for organizations to use reflection to align with environmental and consumer needs.

To be able to cultivate true online communities, trust has to be established with individual community members. Organizations can start this process by using Luhmann's concept of reflection. Once they understand the company from the perspective of the consumer, organizations can develop a willingness to promote their customers' best interests. Finally, they can develop customer service programs that demonstrate their commitment to these interests. If these three things can be achieved, the reward will be a thriving online community filled with engaged consumers.

Applying Design to Customer Communities: Two Examples

The Nestlé Debacle

Nestlé felt the full brunt of the dyadic communication shift in 2010. Nestlé was under fire by activist groups due to the inconsistent use of fair trade palm oil, among other complaints. In 2010, Nestlé Facebook fans begin using altered Nestlé logos to depict environmental damage as their profile picture When the users posted comments on Nestlé's fan page the altered logos were visible to anyone that viewed their comment. The altered picture could not be deleted by Nestlé, since it was the user's profile photo. This meant that Nestlé's 90,000 Facebook fans had the opportunity to see the

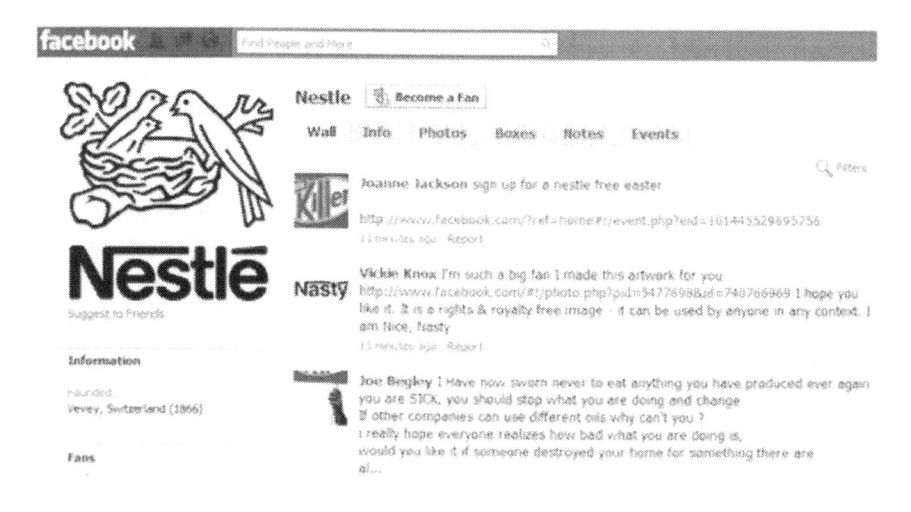

Screenshot of Nestlé's Facebook Fan Page, March 2010

altered logo and learn more about the palm oil fair trade dispute that was affecting Nestlé.

On March 19, 2010 the company's Facebook moderator took it upon himself/herself to inform fans that if they altered Nestlé's logo in any way and posted it as their profile picture they would be deleted from the fan page.

To make matters worse, the moderator continued to argue with the fans as the comment thread grew to over 100 posts commenting, "Thanks for the lesson in manners. Consider yourself embraced. But it's our page, we set the rules, it was ever thus." Finally, the moderator posted a link to an article about proper branding guidelines.

Although Nestlé did not make an official statement, the last comment on March 20, was, "Social media: As you can see we are learning as we go. Thanks for the comments." Despite the apology, Facebook fans began declarations of boycotting the product and people also turned to Twitter to voice their frustrations. What was once an activist issue regarding product ingredients, turned into a global PR crisis overnight (York & Patel, 2010).

Using Luhmann's Communication Cycles observers might notice how Nestlé employed an aggressive communication style toward its Facebook fans in a medium where fans expect the ability to engage in a conversation. The aggressive style continued to repeat itself creating dissonance. The dissonance originated because Nestlé and the public were basing the use of Facebook fan pages on different foundational ideas. Nestlé believed it "owned" the page and, therefore, had the right to make rules governing its use. Yet, the public believed the page was an open forum that Nestlé created to engage in conversation with consumers.

Nestlé misinterpreted the spirit of social media communication. Its foundational idea is based in reflexivity. Nestlé was operating using the perspective that the company's worldview was the only truth and that it had the ability to prevent the public from voicing opinions. By asserting this narcissistic view, Nestlé created dissonance ultimately escalating its public relations crisis regarding the use of palm oil.

Information	Nestle sees altered logos
Utterance	Nestle posts on Facebook: Fans with altered logos will be deleted
Understanding	Nestle learns that altered logos advocate against oil use
Information	Nestle reads response about fans' dissatisfaction and boycott
Utterance	Nestle reiterates need to control brand image
Understanding	Nestle learns fans care more about oil than logo
Information	Nestle considers the role of fans in social media
Utterance	Nestle emphasizes its inexperience in social media
Understanding	Nestle realizes mistake

Luhmann's Dynamics of Circular Communication
A possible representation of Nestle corporate perspective (above), and
A corresponding possible representation of Nestle consumer perspective (below)

Information	Activists learn about limited use of fair trade palm oil
Utterance	Activists retaliate using Facebook altered photos
Understanding	Other Nestle fans see photos and learn about oil use
Information	Fans receive deletion threat from Nestle over altered logos
Utterance	Fans retaliate with talks of boycott and use Twitter
Understanding	Nestle consumers learn of oil use and customer treatment

If, instead, Nestlé employed Luhmann's idea of reflection, the public relations crisis might have been prevented. Reflection would have also enabled Nestlé to view the altered logos as a viewpoint, creating an opportunity to reframe Facebook fans' thoughts by supplying information that showcases the brand's values.

Additionally, Nestlé could have created a dialogue by asking consumers opinion about what was most valuable to them regarding Nestlé's products. This information could have been used to enhance the company's growth thus aligning the organization, the environment, and the public's worldviews.

Best Buy Achieves Innovative Customer Service Design

Best Buy combined social media and customer service in an innovative, transparent way to create a community established on trust. The solution, called Twelpforce, invited employees to sign up on a website with their Twitter handle (example: @agent1223). Whenever they sent a tweet that included the hashtag #twelpforce, their tweet would automatically post to the @Twelpforce Twitter page. Additionally, all Twelpforce tweets were aggregated for search and review at the Best Buy Connect website, www.bbyconnect.appspot.com (Fauscette, 2009).

Through this process, Best Buy used its national 3,000-person retail sales force to constantly answer questions about products (Jarvis, 2011, p 182). Answers are typically linked to detailed, online information. By posting them for everyone to see on both Twitter and the Connect site, Best Buy was able to decrease customer service complaints by 20% in the first year (Jarvis, 2011, p. 183).

Information	*Consumers want information about electronic products*
Utterance	*Consumers express desires to sales associates*
Understanding	*Best Buy recognizes need and develops Twelpforce and Connect*
Information	*Best Buy advertises and begins promotion*
Utterance	*Consumers begin to use the services*
Understanding	*Consumers trust Best Buy to respond to their needs*

Luhmann's Cycles of Communication
A possible representation of a Best Buy, consumer integrated perspective

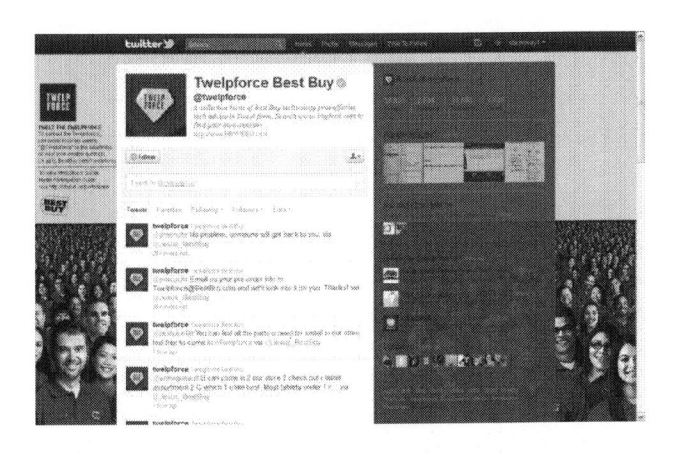

*Screenshots of Best Buy's Twelpforce Twitter Page (above)
and Connect website (below)*

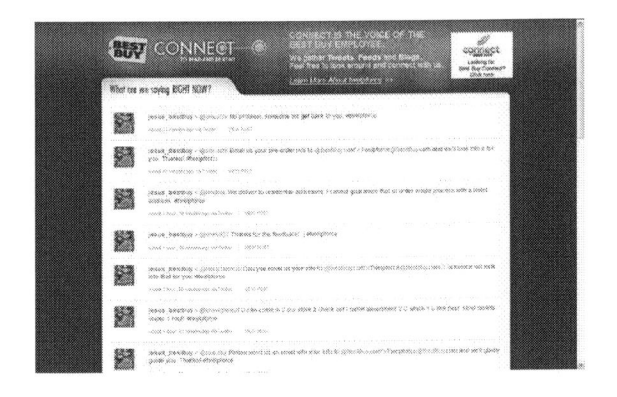

To analyze the success Best Buy engineered, Luhmann's (2000b) Communication Cycle once again provides an excellent framework. Best Buy understood that consumers had a need. They wanted more direct communication with Best Buy personnel who they perceived had useful information regarding electronic products. Best Buy's greatest achievement was its ability to view the organization from the perspective of the customer. This reflective approach allowed the company to orient to the environment based on their consumers' needs.

Best Buy used reflection preemptively, to engage consumers prior to a crisis. Not only did it use Twitter to answer questions, the organization proactively sought ways to aggregate this information for further use. Unlike Nestlé, Best Buy's use of reflection prevented any dissonance from occurring, allowing Best Buy to build trust and create raving fans that engaged in the Twelpforce community.

Another way to view the Twelpforce example is through the framework of informational design. Based on Shedroff's (2009) Information Design Continuum, Best Buy used questions as data that they turned into information by responding via the popular social media site Twitter. Best Buy used this data to create knowledge by aggregating it on the Connect site and using a massive retail sales force as an integrated customer service system. The ability for this to be accessed and shared by other individuals increases wisdom and wins Best Buy huge points with their current and existing customers.

Conclusion & Fundamental Practices

Gone are the days where organizations controlled how consumers communicate with them. The shift has already occurred and consumers are requiring two-way conversations from organizations that they choose to do business with. To be successful, companies must embrace this change and respond. Computer mediated communication is seen as the primary reason that the shift from linear to dyadic communication has occurred. Therefore, companies must create innovative customer service programs that meet consumers in this space. This chapter recommends some fundamental practices for designing online customer service programs. They include:

- Designing platforms and processes that are:
    - Functional - Make it easy to find and use the information you provide.
    - Accessible - Integrate new and existing services to create these platforms.
        - New: Websites and online tools
        - Existing: Facebook, Twitter, YouTube, etc…
    - Interactive – Create ways for consumers to share, respond and converse on information provided.
- Creating & cultivating online communities by providing:
    - Informational value - Share useful information and lots of it.
    - Functional value – Ensure that the design of your site is easy to use.

- o Interaction - Engaging to create and encourage member conversation.
- Establishing trust by fulfilling organizational promises and commitments.
  - o Reflect – View your organization from the point of view of your customer.
  - o Promote - Create customer service programs that promote the needs of your customers.
  - o Respond - If you tout that people can contact you on Twitter be sure to respond.
  - o Protect - If you collect consumer information in exchange for goods or services encrypt and protect it.

For organizations to achieve the dyadic communication model customers are demanding the fundamental aspects of creation, cultivation, design, and trust are critical to establishing new and refining existing online customer service programs. When business communicators use these fundamentals in innovative ways they can increase customer satisfaction and positively impact their business.

References

Andrews, D. C. (2002). Audience-Specific Online Community Design. *Communications of the ACM*, 45(4), 64-68.

Bolkan, S., & Daly, J. A. (2009). Organizational Responses to Consumer Complaints: An Examination of Effective Remediation Tactics. *Journal of Applied Communication Research*, 37(1), 21-39.

Carliner, S. (2000). Physical, cognitive and affective. A three part framework for information design. *Technical Communication* (4), 561-576.

Definitions of information design. (1999). *International Institute for Information Design*. http://members.magnet.at/simlinger-iiid/English-2.html. (this site has changed and this page is no longer available).

Doohwang, L., Hyuk Soo, K., & Jung Kyu, K. (2011). The Impact of Online Brand Community Type on Consumer's Community Engagement Behaviors: Consumer-Created vs. Marketer-Created Online Brand Community in Online Social-Networking Web Sites. *CyberPsychology, Behavior & Social Networking*, 14(1/2), 59-63.

Eliason, F. (Oct. 2011) Social Media Customer Service Failure. http://www.briansolis.com/2011/10/social-media-customer-service-is-a-failure/

Fauscette, M. (Oct. 5, 2009). Twitter As A Customer Service Game Changer... Best Buy's Twelpforce. Social Media Today. http://socialmediatoday.com/index.php?q=SMC/129963

Gunawardena, C. N., Hermans, M., Sanchez, D., Richmond, C., Bohley, M., & Tuttle, R. (2009). A theoretical framework for building online communities of practice with social networking tools. *Educational Media International*, 46(1), 3-16.

Horn, R. "Information Design: Emergence of a New Profession." In Jacobson, R., Ed., *Information Design,* Cambridge, Mass: MIT Press, 1999.

Jarvis. G. M. (Nov. 16, 2011). U.S. economic data encouraging, but Europe muddying the picture. http://articles.chicagotribune.com/2011-11-16/business/ct-biz-1116-gail-20111116_1_fund-managers-electronics-and-appliance-stores-retail-sales.

Jarvis. J. (2011). *Private Parts*. Simon & Schuster; New York, NY.

Liao, C., Liu, C., Liu, Y., To, P., & Lin, H. (2011). Applying the Expectancy Disconfirmation and Regret Theories to Online Consumer Behavior. *CyberPsychology, Behavior & Social Networking*, 14(4), 241-246.

Lee, D. Kim, H. & Kim, J. (2011). The impact of online brand community type on consumer's community engagement behaviors: Consumer-created vs. marketer-created online brand community in online social-networking web sites. *Cyberpsychology, Behavior & Social Networking*, 14 (1-2), 59-63.

Luhmann, N. (2000b). *The reality of mass media*. Cambridge, UK: Polity Press.

Luo, S. & Lee, T. (2011). The influence of trust and usefulness on customer perceptions of e-service quality. *Social Behavior & Personality*, 2011, 39(6), 825-838.

Moliner, B., & Snider, M. (April 2007). Security experts: PlayStation Network breach one of largest ever. USA Today. http://content.usatoday.com/communities/gamehunters/post/2011/04/security-experts-playstation-network-breach-one-of-largest-ever/1

Morgan, R. M., & Hunt, S. D. (1994). The commitment-trust theory of relationship marketing. *Journal of Marketing*, 58(7), 20-38.

Nestlé to Facebook Fans: Consider Yourself Embraced. *Advertising Age Online.* http://adage.com/adages/post?article_id=142881.

Peters, M. (Nov. 23, 2010). Three Examples of Stellar Social Media Customer Service. Mashable. http://mashable.com/2010/11/23/customer-service-award/

Rosenbloom, A. (2000). Trusting Technology. *Communications of the ACM,* 43(12), 30-32.

Schriver, K. (2001) "Response in 'What's in a Name.'" *Design Matters* 5: 8

Shu-Fang, L., & Tzai-Zang, L. (2011). The influence of trust and usefulness on customer perceptions of e-service quality. *Social Behavior & Personality: An International Journal,* 39(6), 825-838.

Solis B. (2012) *The End of Business As Usual.* John Wiley & Sons Inc., Hoboken, NJ.

Solis, B. (Oct. 2011). Social Media's Impending Flood of Customer Unlikes and Unfollows. http://www.briansolis.com/2011/10/social-medias-impending-flood-of-customer-unlikes-and-unfollows/

Turner, J., & Oakes, P. (1986). The significance of the social identity concept for social psychology with reference to individualism, interactionism and social influence. *British Journal of Social Psychology* 25 (3): 237-252.

Williams, S. (2007). User experience design for technical communication: expanding our notions of quality information design.

Xiao-Ling, J., Lee, M. O., & Cheung, C. K. (2010). Predicting continuance in online communities: model development and empirical test. *Behaviour & Information Technology,* 29(4), 383-394.

York, E.B., & Patel, K. (2010). Nestle to Facebook Fans: Consider Yourself Embraced. *Advertising Age Online.* http://adage.com/adages/post?article_id=142881.

About the Author

Kristen Bostedo-Conway is a Marketing Executive in the Charlotte, NC area with more than 12 years of brand management, direct marketing and new media experience. Bostedo-Conway is the recipient of the 2011 eHealthcare Leadership Award for best, integrated marketing campaign and the 2007 Exhibitor All Star Award in addition to other local and regional marketing and communication honors. She has written articles for the marketing trade publication Exhibitor Magazine, and recently co-authored (with Dr. John McArthur) a research study presented at the National Communication Association's 2011 Convention in New Orleans, LA entitled *An exploration of the relationship between Twitter use and student perceptions of teacher behaviors*.

Bostedo-Conway holds a BA in Mass and Human Communication with a minor in marketing from Meredith College and is scheduled to complete her MA in Strategic Communication at Queens University of Charlotte in 2012. Follow her blog *It's A Social Media World* at www.kbconway.com or connect with her on Twitter @kbconway1.

Kristen Bostedo-Conway

Voicing a Campus Icon:
Twitter, a bronze goddess, and hyperlocal community engagement

John A. McArthur

Outlets for hyperlocal news, entertainment, and education have been springing up from grassroots movements and spearheaded by mass media sources nationwide (Shaw, 2007; Thomas, 2008). Blogs, social networking, and other participatory digital media have allowed the instantaneous broadcast of personal, public messages. These tools are utilized by mass media, regional governments, local public figures, and private citizens. But to what end?

McArthur (2011) argues that in digital spaces, some serve as town criers by advancing the news of the day. Others are costermongers peddling their wares. Some become village idiots, making jokes or serving as one. And still others are citizens, listening to the cacophony of voices in hopes of discerning the differences between the three. In all four circumstances, the people of a community are both listening and speaking.

Listening and speaking in the digital space are at once a challenge of production and consumption. Fleming (2010) argues that "the Cronkite-era of the 'trusted' news source is over. In its place is a free-speech free-for-all online" (pp. 143-144). Through a study involving media literacy curricula, Fleming asserts that the key to operating in this free-for-all is "building more critical habits of mind" (p. 143). By this, Fleming means developing the ability to discern between media texts and reflect on personal media use.

Robison (2010) expands this idea: "New media literacies are about understanding and producing meaning, but they are also about participating in media communities, thereby offering context to what is produced and what it means" (p. 197). This expansion integrates the ideas of participation in a community into the literacy skills of meaning-making and critical reflection. When people engage in discussions together, they become part of a community of interest.

This chapter seeks to investigate communities of interest that can be established in digital spaces. To better understand this concept, it provides a tangible example to demonstrate the ways that information design and digital media might combine to become a viable resource for hyperlocal community engagement.

Therefore, this chapter will assert that using a designed object, such as a statue, and combining it with the digital media tool of Twitter, might create and develop a hyperlocal community of interest. To make this claim, this study will explore the eclectic, but somehow related, pieces of this combination: information design, digital media, and hyperlocal community (one characterized by extreme, focused localization or a specific geographic area). To bring these ideas together, the study concludes with one specific case study – the hyperlocal community that surrounds the tweeting statue of Diana at Queens University of Charlotte.

Information Design and Digital Media

Experiencing Information

Recent scholarship in information design and related fields (Albers & Mazur, 2003; Carliner, 2001; Csikszentmihalyi, 1990; Jordan, 2000; Kress and van Leeuwen, 2001; Norman, 2005; Shedroff, 2001; Wurman, 2000) demonstrates the need for a consideration of user-experience in the design process (for an expanded review of this claim, see Williams, 2007). The design of information results in specific outcomes for users who experience the information.

One claim of the information design field emerges as specifically important to this chapter: a user's experience of a designed object creates responses that are emotional and cognitive. Norman's (2005) *Emotional Design: Why we love (or hate) everyday things* labels these responses as visceral, behavioral, and reflective. The visceral response is immediate upon first experiencing an object. "We either feel good or bad, relaxed or tense.

Emotions are judgmental and prepare the body accordingly" (p. 13). For Norman, cognition (e.g. the behavioral and reflective responses) comes only after the visceral response has occurred. The behavioral response arises in the use of the object. The object's efficiency and ability to be used for a particular purpose creates a behavioral response. The reflective response arises after the use of the object when the user reflects on and considers the experience.

A few years prior to Norman's *Emotional Design*, Patrick Jordan authored *Designing Pleasurable Products* (2000) which presents a more nuanced view of the responses described by Norman. Defining pleasure as the addition of value or the removal of a need, Jordan categorized four forms of pleasure a user might experience while interacting with an object: (1) ideo-pleasure is the emotion that is derived from personal values; (2) psycho-pleasure is a result of thinking about or reflecting on the object; (3) socio-pleasure comes from the enjoyment of personal relationships; and (4)physio-pleasure is a result of physiological changes in the body from sensory organs(pp. 13-14). For Jordan, the emotional response of the user is crucial in understanding how information design functions. Functionality and usability must be combined with pleasurability to create a clear picture of information design and a user's experience of that design.

Creation Meets Consumption in Digital Media

When applied to digital media, these conversations return to the interplay between information design and media studies: how does the medium impact the message? In 1964, Marshall McLuhan penned *Understanding Media: Extensions of man*. Many of McLuhan's thoughts on media (e.g. "the medium is the message") have become part of the growing lexicon surrounding digital media. McLuhan's observations about media in the 1960s suggest media and the messages they present become intertwined.

McLuhan's importance to this study becomes clear in the notion that man is connected the medium: "The message of the medium is the change of scale or pace or patterns that it introduces into human affairs" (p. 8). The medium is not a separate entity to be assessed apart from the human context in which it exists. Only 3 years following *Understanding Media*, McLuhan (1967) writes, and potentially laments, that "all media work us over completely" (p. 26). This writing suggests that users are not controlling or reflecting on the media available to them. No longer are we simply considering information in the separately oral or written or visual styles. These modes begin to blend together and converge – both in the creative stage and in the consumptive stage.

Kress and van Leeuwen (2001) discuss what they call the four strata of information design: discourse, design, production, and distribution. These four strata deal with the content of communication (discourse and design) and its expression (production and distribution). The discourse is a reflection of the intended content which is molded by design. The production of that content is centered on its physical manifestation. Finally, its distribution is determined by its flow from the author to the audience.

When digital media are involved, these four strata converge (p.41). Simultaneously, the composer is designing, producing, and distributing information in this type of articulation of content through social media. Suddenly the distribution of the information is simple and the author simultaneously considers the information and how that information is received.

Digital Media and Communities of Interest

The question that the medium must resolve for the user is, "Given this information, what do I do now?" To answer this question, each medium provides its own set of semiotics, signs which aid the user in deriving meaning (Gee, 2007). These internal and external signs are built into the content, distribution, and user experience of the medium in question.

Gee (2007) calls these internal and external design issues "grammars." An object's internal design grammar refers to its structure, content, and medium (all typically chosen by its designer). Its external design is situated around the active use of that object. For example, Gee frames this in terms of video games: Whereas the internal design grammar of a video game – things like the plot, imagery, and path of the game – is determined by the game's designers, "people who play, review, and discuss such games, as well as those who design and produce them, shape the external design grammar…through their ongoing social interaction" (p. 31). The community of interest that surrounds the game, in this case, shapes the way that people use, understand, and apply the game. Their conversations and information sharing create and modify the game's external design grammar.

Thereby, becoming acquainted with a medium is a first step toward meaning-making and meaning-production within that medium. It is the first step in becoming a part of the community of interest surrounding an idea or object.

Designing in and Using Twitter

Before looking at the community of interest (the hyperlocal community), this chapter understanding the medium that supports this community: Twitter. According to its own website, Twitter asks users to answer the question "What's happening?" in 140 characters or less. These updates are called *tweets*. These tweets are posted on the author's Twitter homepage and are sent to the pages of any readers who are *following* the author. This micro-blog inspires readers and writers to share both the profound and the mundane about their lives.

Early critics and skeptics of Twitter have suggested that the service is a waste of time and an indicator of a bored culture. In a rebuttal to these critics, *Wired Magazine's* Clive Thompson (2007) asks, "So why has Twitter been so misunderstood?" He answers, "Because it's experiential. Scrolling through random Twitter messages can't explain the appeal. You have to *do* it" (para. 9). According to Thompson, Twitter offers a learning and knowing opportunity for its users to know one another and to share information. Educator Vance Stevens (2008) expands upon this claim:

> What we're talking about here is just-in-time informal learning, social networking, low affective filters, a playground for knowledge workers where you can "follow" almost anyone you choose and enjoy his or her 140 character musings, often with a provocative URL to explore, from time to time, day to day, and even minute to minute. These gems of genuine interest are lodged in a matrix of emerging personalities that are themselves interesting. The result is an engaging mix of personality and professionalism. (p. 4)

Both Thompson and Stevens indicate that Twitter holds opportunities for learning in terms of both knowledge and expression. Moreover, Stein (2009) suggests that this learning takes the form of a cultural dialogue: "Readers thus encounter a synthesis of layers, multiauthored at the intersection of multiple interfaces. This interplay between interfaces creates an ever-changing, decentralized landscape of cultural conversation" (p. 4). These layers of content, expression, authorship, and distribution are combined in multiple ways, reflecting the concepts of McLuhan (1964) and Kress and van Leeuwen (2001) stated earlier in this study. This cultural conversation is not solely the result of social networking, but also the result of information (content: discourse and design) and its delivery (expression: production and distribution) through Twitter.

Twitter and other social networking sites have generated an ongoing discussion in academic circles, across business arenas, and throughout traditional media. At the same time that *The New York Times* hired its first editor for social media, news organizations worldwide reported on the claim of Dr. Tracy Alloway (2009), a scholar and researcher of working memory, that Twitter may adversely affect memory. Even as businesses across the globe are sending employees to social media seminars, marketing-analysis outfit Pearanalytics (2009) conducted a study of Twitter posts indicating that 40% of all tweets are "pointless babble" (p. 5). And educators around the nation are trying to determine if they should use Twitter in class, or ignore it all together (Fischman, 2009).

Early research into Twitter (see Huberman, Romero, & Wu, 2008), suggests that Twitter usage is primarily centered around information acquisition and exchange, rather than relationship or network building. Ellcessor (2009) clarifies the claim that Twitter is a strictly broadcast medium, indicating that the connection between people as writers and followers defines the medium. Ellcessor points out that Twitter is unlike other social networking sites (e.g. Facebook, MySpace) which require two users to each agree to share their information before viewing. Twitter, conversely, does not require this reciprocity. The people that a reader follows on Twitter can be anyone of interest: Ashton Kutcher, Oprah Winfrey, or Barack Obama. Ellcessor writes, "Thus, my Facebook friends are people I've known personally. Twitter can be for communicating with people I want to know" (p. 5). Notably, this idea was first conceived by Ellcessor as a tweet.

Hyperlocal Community

Before investigating Twitter's role in developing a single hyperlocal community, this study seeks to define the term. Below are several definitions posed for "hyperlocal" in relation to media impact:

- "Hyperlocal blogs are usually written by community residents and focus on a small geographic area or topic within a community" (Hallett, 2008, p. 25).

- "A hyperlocal news site (also known as a local-local or microsite) is devoted to stories and minutiae of a particular neighborhood, ZIP code or interest group within a certain geographic area" (Shaw, 2007, p. 55).
- "Hyperlocal news is community-focused reporting, once the domain of daily and weekly newspapers. It is here that coverage of high school athletics, civic affairs, and regional weather tops that of global and national events" (Thomas, 2008, p. 21).
- A hyperlocal website "provides coverage of issues that are of real concern here... simple but timely local coverage" (Rector, 2008, p.10).

This study, therefore, might define a "hyperlocal community" as a group of people who have a shared interest in the issues, stories, and minutiae of a small, particular geographic area. "Information must not only be relevant, but also must be hypersegmented and delivered in real time via the Internet and mobile smart phones" (Bry, 2009, p. 20). Pointing to her experience with the San Diego News Network and sites such as Everyblock, Outside.In, Placeblogger, and Patch, Bry suggests that one of the key issues for information relevance in journalism is developing local content.

Gup's (2007) report on the Bucksport (ME) *Enterprise* reveals that hyperlocal newspapers and blogs continue to thrive in a difficult arena for newspapers. Paiser's (2010) review of hyperlocal business ventures suggests that successful local news sites are "outliers" (p. 68). Shaw (2007) offers hyperlocal news as a possible trajectory for niche-building: "In every area, there are unique things, stories that the local paper can dominate" (p.57).

In a 2008 study on local sports media, Schultz and Sheffer argue that local information outlets, like those for local sports, are at a crossroads – in one direction, obsolescence; in the other, reinvention. They suggest that whereas local broadcasts come at a large expense to stations, these broadcasts produce high levels of satisfaction for viewers.

These geographic areas thrive on local information to provide a local connection. Gup (2007) quotes Bucksport, Maine's Sandy Holmes describing her community's hyperlocal paper: "This paper gives the town a voice. Otherwise, it's like a silent movie" (p. 13). The media that create these hyperlocal connections are print media in some cases and digital media in others. Yet, each of these cases shared one thing in common: the community served by hyperlocal media was strengthened.

One Example

This study attempted to make the case that information design through digital media has the opportunity to engage users, and to create pockets of hyperlocal communities within an increasingly global world. To assess and reinforce this claim, this chapter concludes with one example: the tweeting statue of Diana, Goddess of the Hunt, that resides in the Diana Courtyard at Queens University of Charlotte in Charlotte, North Carolina. The bronze statue stands in the middle of a circular fountain in a highly-trafficked common area of campus. The following piece provides a good synopsis of the history of Diana as an icon on the Queens University of Charlotte campus. As an article that was featured on the Queens website, it is at once a descriptor of the project and part of the conversation (external design grammar) that surrounds the statue:

> Amidst elements that threaten to oxidize, cleanse, sear and scar, the bronze statue of *Young Diana* nobly stands, keeping watch over those who pass her by. Cast by renowned sculptor Anna Hyatt Huntington in 1924, the bronze was a gift to the university from the artist herself in 1940. This year, Diana celebrates her seventieth anniversary as a fixture on the idyllic Queens University of Charlotte campus.
>
> Over the past seven decades, she watched as her beloved Queens grew, fashioning itself into a leading comprehensive university. She famously donned a tie to welcome the first resident men onto campus in the 1980s. She remained the college's stalwart icon in a transition from small liberal arts college to thriving university. And, in her prominent location in the (appropriately-named) Diana courtyard, she is, perhaps, the most photographed location on the Myers Park campus.
>
> The silent observer of her domain, Diana has often served as a gathering site, a model, an element in art projects, and a marketing icon for the institution and her students. And in 2009, Diana combined all of those roles together as she began speaking for

herself, through the advancing technology of Twitter (@QueensDiana, Diana's Twitter profile).

A tweeting statue is not an original idea. A pair of enormous lions tweet about the events in and around the Art Institute of Chicago (@ChicagoLions). The Statue of Liberty shares insights and information for visitors (@StatueLibrtyNPS). The Eric Morcambe statue in Lancashire, England even tweets the weather twice a day for the convenience of locals (@ericsstatue). Yet, Diana is a hyperlocal example of the type of interaction that Twitter and other social media can provide, even among the inanimate.

> Keeping watch over the comings and goings of my Royals.
>
> QueensDiana
> Diana at Queens

@QueensDiana's first tweet, November 17, 2009

In her early days on Twitter, Diana socialized primarily with other statues and the professors and staff at Queens University of Charlotte (@QueensUniv), but her appeal quickly drew the attention of Charlotteans. In a city influenced heavily by social media, she was a fast friend for area social media leaders, even tweeting out photos at *The Charlotte Observer*'s first Social Media Conference. As a result, the kings of Twitter's inanimate beasts - the Art Institute's Lions - crowned her "Queen of the Inanimate Twitterverse."

The true identity of the person(s) behind @QueensDiana has been a well-kept secret in her first year of social media fame, but those who follow her tweets know that she is more than a marketing ploy or info-bot. She tweets according to the day, the mood, and the circumstances of life at Queens University of Charlotte. She shares anecdotes of love, faith, strength, and wisdom; but more importantly, she connects with her followers directly, often re-tweeting their ideas or the events they think are important.

On campus, she has always been a physical site for making connections. Perhaps it is fitting that her role in the digital world is no different. (McArthur, 2010)

Diana's tweets generally surround four major areas: (1) inspiration and wisdom, often as quotes that reflect the time, day, or life of the university; (2) updates about the events occurring on campus; (3) conversations with Queens students, faculty, staff, visitors, and community members; and (4) re-tweets of interesting thoughts and ideas of students, faculty, and staff at Queens. These four areas created a follower base of 1200 people over Diana's first year and outpaced the University's official Twitter presence (@QueensUniv) during that time.

To illustrate the types of hyperlocal engagement created by Diana on Twitter, this study turns to user responses. On Twitter, responses can be directed to any user through the insertion of that user's Twitter username into the text of a tweet. Inserting "@QueensDiana" into a tweet, for example, links readers to the statue's Twitter page and creates a searchable conversation that can be monitored. Using a content analysis of these mentions on Twitter, this study identified mentions that suggest a relationship to the visceral, behavioral, and reflective responses that Norman (2005) associated with information design.

Users' visceral response to @QueensDiana

The visceral response that users have to a tweet is perhaps the most difficult to assess. As noted previously, this response occurs before cognition starts. Quick, impulsive tweets might be the most likely window into this type of response to Diana. Some of @QueensDiana's followers give a glimpse into their visceral responses. Below, tweets from @chelseylance and @Mikeyef demonstrate the conversation that occurred and an identified response, directed to the statue.

> **QueensDiana**
> Trying to catch snowflakes on my tongue. #ohOMG
>
> **@chelseylance**
> @QueensDiana That was one of the cutest tweets I've ever seen.
>
> **QueensDiana**
> A few favorite Royals #FF @mikewith @NattyMarZ @Mikeyef @JAMcArthur @owenshill @SBJones11 and introducing @Everettlibrary
>
> **@Mikeyef**
> @QueensDiana thanks diana making me smile!

In both cases, the follower reports some emotional response to a tweet made by Diana. In the tweet, below, @TheReal_Maximus shares a visceral response as well:

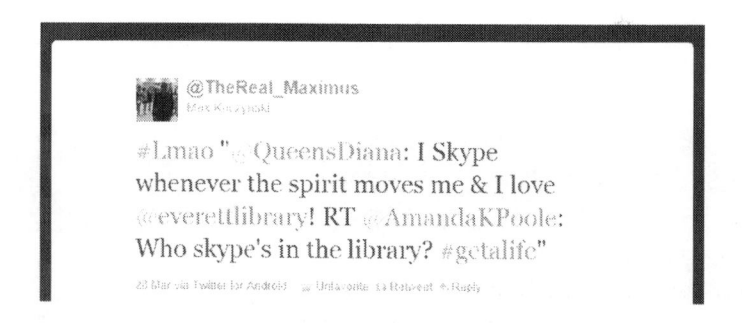

> **@TheReal_Maximus**
> #Lmao " @QueensDiana: I Skype whenever the spirit moves me & I love @everettlibrary! RT @AmandaKPoole: Who skype's in the library? #getalife"

For those unfamiliar with the language of Twitter, the tweet above indicates that the author is quoting a tweet written by @QueensDiana and has added his reaction: "#Lmao," which stands for "laughing my ass off."

These responses are immediate. They come without reflection or action, but simply as a gut reaction to the statue's tweets. In each case, readers will notice the immediate exchange and interplay between the statue and the follower.

Users' behavioral response to @QueensDiana

Behavioral responses to the tweets of @QueensDiana occur when the follower can be seen interacting with Diana in a physical way. As noted above, a behavioral response occurs during the use of an object. The tweets below reveal that followers, in the process of coming in contact with Diana's physical presence, feel compelled to speak directly to her digitally. The first, from Charlottean @WCooksey, indicates that this visitor to campus has taken a photo of the statue during his visit and tweeted it out.

> **@WCooksey**
> Warren Cooksey
>
> It wouldn't be right if I didn't check in w/ @QueensDiana before leaving. [pic]: http://4sq.com/hkrFJ5
>
> 19 Feb via foursquare · Unfavorite · Retweet · Reply

The second example, from @crowsweed, suggests that this follower has sent a child to a summer camp and has enlisted the statue as a perceived surveillance tool:

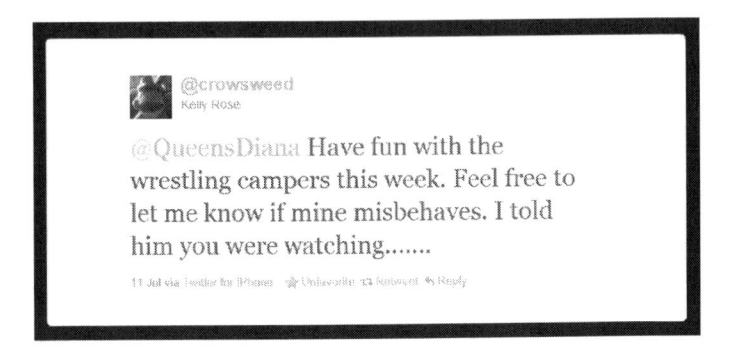

> **@crowsweed**
> Kelly Rose
>
> @QueensDiana Have fun with the wrestling campers this week. Feel free to let me know if mine misbehaves. I told him you were watching.......
>
> 11 Jul via Twitter for iPhone · Unfavorite · Retweet · Reply

This third example indicates that this student swam in the fountain around the statue and relayed her experience through Twitter:

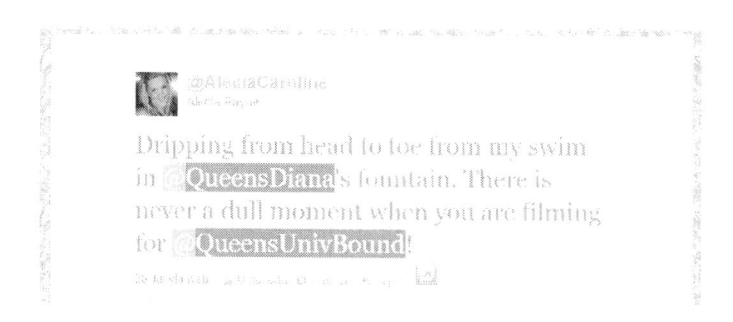

> @AleciaCaroline
> Alecia Bryant
>
> Dripping from head to toe from my swim in @QueensDiana's fountain. There is never a dull moment when you are filming for @QueensUnivBound!

In each of these cases, the followers have combined their experience with the Diana statue as a physical object with their knowledge of Diana's digital presence to create a behavioral response to the statue. These examples suggest that the statue's digital presence has enhanced their behaviors and interaction with the object itself.

As noted previously, Gee (2007) might refer to this behavioral response as the meeting of the internal and external design grammars during the use of the statue. These interchanges look different than the visceral responses noted above. Whereas the visceral responses immediately followed Diana's tweets, behavioral responses occurred in direct interaction with the statue itself and were then displayed on Twitter.

Users' reflective response to @QueensDiana

From a reflective perspective, readers might notice that followers respond to Diana in a variety of ways that signify their understanding of and reflection upon the statue and her tweets.

> @underoak
> Andrew Koewsch
>
> @cbjgreennews So it's AR-tə-miss, descended from earlier ar-TI-mi-te. Morphed by Romans into @queensdiana. How apropos. #hungergames

This first example from @underoak illustrates cognitive reflection about the Greek and Roman mythical history of the goddess Diana (Artemis) and transitions that history using @QueensDiana as an example.

Interestingly, this Twitter account belongs to an area Charlottean who is unaffiliated with Queens, except by geography.

The next example of reflective response to Diana comes from a Queens University of Charlotte alumna who reflects on her own experience as a student:

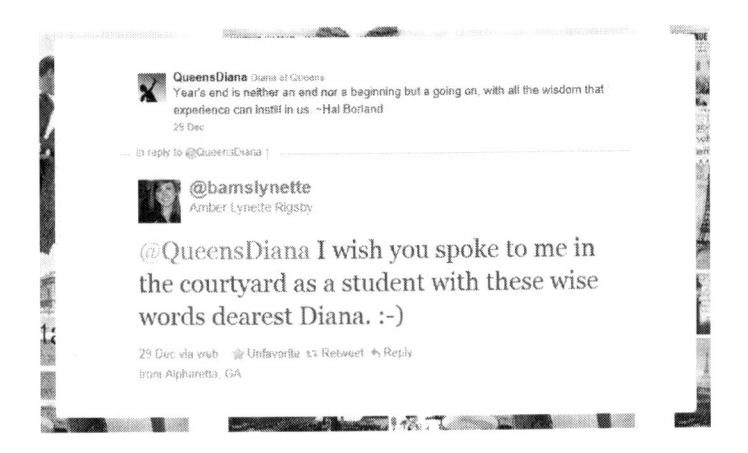

> **QueensDiana** Diana at Queens
> Year's end is neither an end nor a beginning but a going on, with all the wisdom that experience can instill in us. ~Hal Borland
> 29 Dec
>
> in reply to @QueensDiana
>
> **@bamslynette**
> Amber Lynette Rigsby
>
> @QueensDiana I wish you spoke to me in the courtyard as a student with these wise words dearest Diana. :-)
>
> 29 Dec via web ☆ Unfavorite ⇄ Retweet ↩ Reply
> from Alpharetta, GA

Both of the above responses employ a theoretical, cognitive connection between Diana's physical presence and her location in Charlotte and on the campus of the university. Conversely, the next two responses employ critical reflection about Diana's role in Twitter.

> **QueensDiana** Diana at Queens
> @mollyannwarren
> #mentalhealthtweet
> 5 Oct
>
> in reply to @QueensDiana
>
> **@mollyannwarren**
> Molly Warren
>
> @QueensDiana thanks for the mention, Di. Much love to you and your beautiful bronze body.
>
> 🔒 5 Oct via Twitter for iPhone ☆ Unfavorite ↩ Reply

> **QueensDiana**
> That's me! RT ...
>
> **@CarFogle**
> I was retweeted by @QueensDiana fountain yesterday. Highlight of my college career? I think yes. #thatsnotsadatall

Both of these tweets signify a relationship between current students and @QueensDiana – the Twitter account – as opposed to Diana the statue. Both are indicative of the feelings of pride in the Queens community about interaction with Diana on Twitter. Diana is the member of the campus community who has the most Twitter followers, affording her the opportunity to speak for, with, to, and among the various constituencies of the university.

Diana and hyperlocal engagement

Claims about the visceral, behavioral, and reflective responses to Diana are not meant to limit followers and viewers only to their decisions on Twitter. However, it is clear that interacting with Diana on Twitter has heightened their sense of engagement with the statue, and perhaps, therefore with the hyperlocal community of Queens University of Charlotte.

The community within the university and in the surrounding city of Charlotte have adopted Diana as one among the city's "Twitter elite." She is well known by the local social media leaders and is listed on over 100 Charlotte-area lists of influential people.

Nevertheless, she is perhaps best known by the Queens community. She maintains lists of all Queens students, faculty, staff, and alumni on Twitter. She re-tweets their comments, offers encouragement, and shares their stories. Her story is their story – the story of a hyperlocal community tied to the ZIP code 28274.

Could Queens University of Charlotte have a vibrant and engaged hyperlocal community without Diana's tweets? Of course.

Did the hyperlocal community exist on campus before Diana began tweeting? Maybe.

But, does Diana's presence on Twitter deepen or enhance the hyperlocal community that exists on campus?

The examples above suggest that it might. As a site of connection, Diana's physical presence and her digital one add to the engagement of community members at Queens University of Charlotte.

The most telling example of this proposition comes from an outsider to the Queens community:

> **@agracelamb**
> Hannah Baartmans
>
> @QueensDiana I'll be transferring to Queens next fall! I'm a Charlotte native and can't wait to be a Queens Royal :)
>
> 1 Mar via web   ☆ Unfavorite ⇄ Retweet ↰ Reply

In this instance, @agracelamb has noticed the feeling of community surrounding the tweets of this campus statue. From this tweet, readers might infer that knowledge of @QueensDiana on Twitter enhances the feelings of engagement in the university community. This follower sees @QueensDiana as a leader of the community and looks to her for inclusion. And, judging by the interactions occurring on Twitter, she is not alone.

References

Albers, M., & Mazur, B. (Eds.) (2003). *Content and Complexity: Information design in technical communication.* Mahwah, NJ: Lawrence Erlbaum & Associates, Inc.

Alloway, T. (2009). "Social Networking: Bad for your memory?" Retrieved August 2009), from http://tracyalloway.com/index.php/news/

Bry, B. (2009, June). Why local news is no longer proprietary and how this changes the role of the PR professional. *Public Relations Tactics.* 20.

Carliner, S. (2000). Physical, cognitive, & affective: A three-part framework for information design. *Technical Communication.* 561-576.

Csikszentmihalyi, M. (1990). *Flow: The Psychology of Optimal Experience*. New York: Harper & Row Publishers.

Ellcessor, L. (2009). "People I want to know: Twitter, celebrity and social connection." *FlowTV*, 9.14, Retrieved May 2009, from http://flowtv.org/?p=3954

Fleming, J. (2010). "Truthiness" and Trust: News media literacy strategies in the digital age. In K. Tyner (Ed.), *Media Literacy: New agendas in communication* (pp. 124-146). New York: Routledge.

Fischman, J. (2009) Can Twitter turn students into better writers? The Wired Campus. *The Chronicle of Higher Education*. Retrieved August 2009, from http://chronicle.com/blogPost/Can-Twitter-Turn-Students-Into/7874/

Gee, J. P. (2007). *What Video Games Have to Teach Us about Learning and Literacy*. New York: Palgrave Macmillan.

Gup, T. (2007, Oct./Nov.). Covering 'the center of the known universe.' *American Journalism Review*. 12-13.

Hallett, J. (2008, May). In through the back door: Using blogs to reach traditional media. *Public Relations Tactics*. 25.

Huberman, B. A., Romero, D. M., and Wu, F. (2008). "Social Networks that Matter: Twitter Under the Microscope." Social Science Research Network, Working Paper Series. Retrieved May 2009, from http://ssrn.com/abstract=1313405

Jordan, P. A. (2000). *Designing Pleasurable Products*. London: Taylor & Francis, Inc.

Kress, G., & van Leeuwen, T. (2001). *Multimodal Discourse: The modes and media of contemporary communication*. London: Hodder-Arnold.

McArthur, J. A. (2010). Diana, Queen of the Inanimate Twitterverse. Retrieved October 2010, from http://www.queens.edu/Life-on-Campus/Spotlight-Stories/Diana-queen-of-the-inanimate-Twitterverse.html

McArthur, J. A. (2011, Sept. 30). Town Crier? Village Idiot? We each have role in public space [Op-Ed]. *Charlotte Observer*, 10A.

McLuhan, M. (1964). *Understanding Media: The Extensions of Man*. Chicago :McGraw-Hill.

McLuhan, M. (1967). *The Medium is the MASSAGE*. New York: Random House - Bantam Books.

Norman, D. A. (2005). *Emotional Design: Why we love (or hate) everyday things*. New York: Basic Books.

Paiser, B. (2010). The Hazards of Hyperlocal: Why neighborhood news online is a dicey proposition. *American Journalism Review.* 68.

Pearanalytics (2009) Twitter Study, August 2009. Retrieved August 2009, from http://www.pearanalytics.com/wp-content/uploads/2009/08/Twitter-Study-August-2009.pdf

Rector, K. (2008, Aug./Sept.). Voice in the Wilderness. *American Journalism Review.* 10-11.

Robison, A. (2010). New Media Literacies by Design. In K. Tyner (Ed.), *Media Literacy: New agendas in communication* (pp. 192-208). New York: Routledge.

Schultz, B. & Shaffer, M. L. (2008). Left Behind: Local television and the community of sport. *Western Journal of Communication, 72* (2), 180-195.

Shaw, D. (2007, April/May). Really Local. *American Journalism Review.*54-57.

Shedroff, N. (2001). *Experience Design 1*. Indianapolis, IN: New Riders Publishing.

Stein, L. (2009). It's contagious: Twitter and the palimpsest of authorhip. *FlowTV*, 9.14, Retrieved May 2009, from http://flowtv.org/?p=3922

Stevens, V. (2008). Trial by Twitter: The rise and slide of the year's most viral micro-blogging platform. *Teaching English as a Second or Foreign Language, 12* (1). Retrieved May 2009, from http://www.tesl-ej.org/ej45/int.pdf

Thomas, L. (2008, July). From mass to me: Hyperlocal television caters to communities. *Public Relations Tactics.* 21.

Thompson, C. (2007, June 26). Clive Thompson on how Twitter creates a social sixth sense. *Wired Magazine, 15.07*. Retrieved May 2009, from http://www.wired.com/techbiz/media/magazine/15-07/st_thompson

Twitter.com (2009). "Twitter." Retrieved May 2009, from http://twitter.com/about#about

Williams, S. D. (2007). User experience design for technical communication: Expanding our notions of quality information design. *Proceedings of the Annual Meeting of the IEEE Professional Communication Society.*

Wurman, R. S. (1997). *Information Architects*. New York, NY: Watson-Guptill Publications.

Images

All images are screenshots of original public tweets captured from @QueensDiana's favorite tweets, available at http://www.twitter.com/queensdiana/favorites .

About the Author

John A. McArthur is a professor and researcher of user-experience design, proxemics (the communicativity of space), and the role of technology and media design in society. He focuses much of his study on using these interests for successful instructional practice. Dr. McArthur's current research includes studies of the ways that we produce and distribute information using the various platforms of medium and modality, including digital environments, speeches, print documents, physical space, and social media.

A member of the faculty of the James L. Knight School of Communication at Queens University of Charlotte, Dr. McArthur serves as the Director of Undergraduate Programs for the school. He is a member and active presenter in the National Communication Association (NCA) and sits on the national SMCEDU (Social Media and Education) Advisory Board. He can be reached on Twitter @JAMcArthur or through his website: http://jamcarthur.com.

A version of this chapter was juried, accepted for presentation, and presented at the 2011 National Communication Association National Convention in New Orleans, Louisiana.

John A. McArthur

Finding Community through Blogging

Jennifer L. Hull

On Wednesday, May 12, 2010 my normal and healthy pregnancy was disrupted. At 32 weeks, I woke up with a little bleeding. As I read my pregnancy book to determine my own diagnosis, I remained calmed. An hour later, I was in the doctor's office being told I was in pre-term labor. My normal and healthy pregnancy was no longer going to (my) plan.

I called my husband who met me on the maternity floor about 10 minutes after I spoke to him on the phone. I was immediately hooked up to machines to stop labor and injected with steroids to strengthen my unborn daughter's lungs. Luckily, the doctor and nurses were able to stop labor.

The next set of news my doctor delivered ended up being my first orders as a new mother. I was told I had to be on bed rest at the hospital, since my water did break and I was now considered a high-risk pregnancy. The risk of infection was a possibility, so I had to be monitored around the clock. The goal was to get my daughter to 34 weeks. Two more weeks meant two more weeks of growing inside me that she needed. After that, the risk of infection outweighed the benefits of staying in the womb. Thankfully, my daughter was born two weeks later. Albeit tiny, she was healthy.

During those two weeks on bed rest and the days after her birth in the Neonatal Intensive Care Unit, friends and family members wanted up-to-date information about our progress. For me however, the thought of mass e-mailing seemed impersonal. The idea of engaging in repeated phone conversations to share the daily improvements or set-backs seemed exhausting. Additionally, the idea of posting my daughter's progress on Facebook seemed trite and inappropriate. What I was searching for and figured out a year later was the digital tool I needed – a blog.

At the time, developing a new blog would have been a daunting task. I was too busy concentrating on my daughter to design a website. Plus, a blog seemed to be open for all-to-see. I was not ready to share my private experience with the world but I still needed a way to nurture a support group that my family needed during our health crisis.

***

This chapter will examine how a specific digital tool, a blog, can create a sense of community among a virtual world of mothers, fathers, friends, family and, potentially, complete strangers. First, the chapter will explain what blogs are, how they are designed, and the role of this digital tool in storytelling. Using information design theory, the chapter will turn to CaringBridge.org, a website that hosts individual health blogs, to examine how the design of a CaringBridge blog sets the template for people going through a health crisis, so that they do not have to worry about the set-up and design of their personal blog. All they need to focus on is their story, their progress, their healing. Then, the chapter will explore how these blogs develop a social support community of family and friends during a health crisis. Finally, the chapter will assert that, through this engagement bloggers are able to communicate their journeys to their community of loves ones, and they are able to heal knowing that they have a community of digital support even if their physical family is miles away.

The Digital Tool: Blogs

The Internet is a powerful tool that can provide knowledge and community to a single person who has access to a computer and Internet connection. The World Wide Web has dramatically changed since its public inception in 1994. Web 1.0 turned into Web 2.0 when user-generated content became king (Ancker et al., 2009). "Web 2.0 enables 'regular' people…to create content online" (Sarasohn-Kahn, 2008, p. 2). This new version of the Web has "transform[ed] Internet communication from one-way (publication by a relatively small number of experts and advertisers) to multiway (with millions of consumers and small organizations using easy-to-use software to create, share, aggregate, and edit content)" (Ancker et al., 2009, p. 39). This "multiway" communication is taking place in several ways online; one of them being blogging.

As of November 2011, the blogosphere had over 177 million public blogs (Blogpulse, 2011). Many authors have their own definitions for blogs, but it boils down to this: a blog is "a webpage with minimal to no external editing, providing online commentary, periodically updated and presented in reverse chronological order, with hyperlinks to other online sources" (McKenna, 2007, p. 210). This means a blog is a digital tool where anyone can write their thoughts, feelings, or opinions. The writer is also the editor of the blog.

Blogs are written on every subject – politics, education, health, decorating, parenting and more. The list could go on and on. "The blogosphere consists of multiple forms of expression that range from intimate confessions aimed at a few people to journalistic and scholarly writings that attract large number of readers" (Kouper, 2010, p. 2).

In 2010, the Associated Press acknowledged that blogs could be credible news sources and would begin to cite them in news articles (Dugan, 2010). This gives bloggers clout and reinforces the credibility of their writing, making the bloggers more responsible writers (Dugan, 2010). The large number of blogs in the blogosphere along with the AP's acceptance of blogs as trustworthy sources of information demonstrates the power of blogs today.

Blog designs typically follow a general pattern. The layout is simple: a header, a wall of posts, and a general section or page which can include other features like a small biography on the author, archives, and a blog roll. A blog roll is a list of recommended sites that the author believes to be important. These sites are linked to the blog. Linking to other credible blogs can make a blog appear more authoritative and also provides additional information for the reader (Miller & Pole, 2010).

Blog content includes text and can include photographs, videos or audio clips (Price, 2010, p. 35). An archive section is usually located on the right hand side of the blog and houses a search capability for all past entries (Miller & Pole, 2010). This design feature helps the reader find a relevant story or re-read a previous entry. Underneath each blog entry is a comments section where readers can leave their comments about the post.

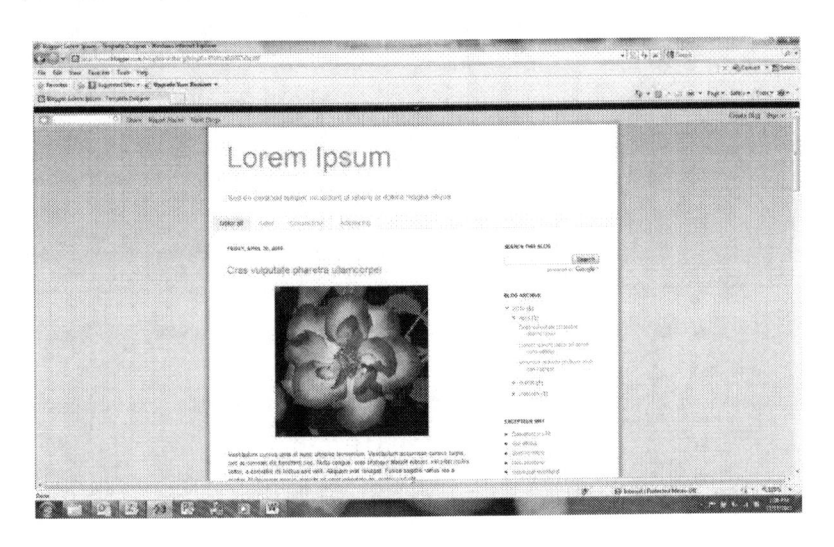

Example of a blog template, in this screenshot from www.blogger.com

In the late 1990s when a large portion of the online population became content creators, the blogosphere exploded (Miller & Pole, 2010). "Web content was no longer the sole province of the big portals and media companies," which meant that anyone with a computer and Internet access could share their thoughts to the World Wide Web (Funk, 2008, p. 3). Free blogging software programs such as Blogger or WordPress have made it easier for novice users to create and share their story for a community on the Internet. "The purpose [of a blog] is to disseminate information and to share experiences or ideas with others" (Price, 2010, p. 35). Blogs can provide relevant and reliable information to a community in an easy-to-read format.

Blogs & Information Design

Within the blogging community, some common practices define how a typical blog is designed. A blog will have a heading, blog entries, an archive section, a comments section and a blog roll. Some of these design features are optional, but they all set the foundation for the blog and for the user-experience. Along with figuring out the content, the author will also take the time to develop the aesthetics and layout of the blog.

Information design is defined as "the defining, planning, and shaping of the contents of a message and the environments it is presented in with the intention of achieving particular objectives in relations to the needs of users"

(Williams, 2007, p. 1). This means taking information and shaping it in a way for people to understand and use. Information designers take time to think about the information, the environment into which it will be placed, the user and the user's experience. The end goal is for the user to be able to process the information easily and effectively. The way a blog has been designed by the author and the experience understood and shared by the reader are both part of a blog's design.

The rules the author followed to create a blog are called its internal design grammar. James Paul Gee, who investigates design and learning, defines internal design grammar as "principles and patterns...in which one can recognize what is and what is not acceptable or typical content in a semiotic domain" (2003, p. 30). Within a blog this means how a blog is designed and the "rules" set forth by the blog's design. For example, a reader may be able to navigate through various posts and click on links within a post, but not be able to export photos from a post. These rules are the choices of the blog designer.

The experience understood and shared by the blogging community is called the external design grammar. Gee defines this as "the principles and patterns...in which one can recognize what is and what is not acceptable or typical social practice[s] and identity in regard to the affinity group associated with a semiotic domain" (2003, p. 30). In this case, a blogging community creates a conversation on a blog because they understand the nuances of the blog, the rules, and the identity and actions of the author and followers. The blogging community also knows how to act with one another and what are correct social behaviors. For example, external design grammar includes the online and off-line conversations that surround the material included on the blog.

The concept of internal and external design grammars ground this section in information design because the grammars showcase the importance of how being literate in the blogging domain creates a more meaningful experience with the author and community.

Internal Design Grammar: Designing a blog

Through the lens of information design, blogs might be worthwhile avenues for information distribution because (1) they are simple to read; (2) they can be easily updated in real time; (3) they are interactive; and (4) they are vehicles for storytelling.

The four main features of a blog – header, posts, comments and archive – are so well-organized that it is easy to follow even if someone is new to a blog. In *The Laws of Simplicity*, John Maeda might argue that an uncomplicated layout is powerful because it is organized well (2006, p. 11). Through a simple layout of header, blog roll, archives and comment section, the actual format does not clutter the page. This clean layout is organized and easy-to-read. The layout helps the reader know exactly where to go and what to do in each section of the blog. The design of the blog is so simple that a newcomer to the blogosphere could easily figure out how it works. This straightforward approach helps build a community because it does not deter anyone from giving up.

Along with the easy-to-read format, the daily update of a blog facilitates the expansion of a community. "In making regular entries (postings) on the blog, the blogger tries to develop a dialogue with others" (Price, 2010, p. 35). Daily updates keep a blog fresh and current. If the blogger poses a question in a post, then the followers can respond and discuss among one another in the comment section. This discourse facilitates a discussion among the community and determines the acceptable social behaviors within the group.

Another key aspect of the blog is how it is written. Since a blog can act as an online journal, this story-telling helps bring people together because they are familiar with the format. The blog entries are laid out in reverse chronological order, but they still tell a story – like a daily journal. "Storytelling is one of the oldest experiences and still one of the most powerful because it organizes information in a way that allows us, usually, to draw personal meaning and create knowledge" (Shedroff, 2009, p. 208). In storytelling there is a beginning, middle and end. The same goes for a blog, but the order is viewed differently on-screen. The current story is posted first, and all the stories that came before it are posted underneath or archived. People enjoy stories and are familiar with this format, so again, it helps the reader feel at ease when navigating through the blog.

Nathan Shedroff (2009) states, "Information is really data transformed into something more valuable by building context around it so that it becomes understandable" (p. 34). As Henry Jenkins (2006) discusses how media, culture and collective intelligence are converging, he states, "Each of us constructs our own personal mythology from bits and fragments of information extracted from the media flow and transformed into resources through which we make sense of our everyday lives" (p. 4-5). Shedroff's and

Jenkins' arguments are that we build meaning from our own experiences. Through our experiences and sharing of those experiences creates information and ultimately wisdom (Shedroff, 2009). A blog can create wisdom by allowing the blogger to share his personal story with his community. For example, someone who shares their health journey via a blog provides information that turns into knowledge for their family and friends. Sharing through a blog has created a way for a community to collectively gain the knowledge contained on the blog.

Shedroff (2009) continues by saying "we have learned from information design that structure, itself, has meaning" a blog's structure, an online journal, has created meaning for the readers (p. 34). Associating a blog to a journal gives the blog more authenticity. A journal is personal and a blog can be too. Therefore, the actual structure of daily journaling provides meaning to the blogging experience, since journaling is a private and intimate affair. This act makes blogging personal but also supports a community's engagement because of the very nature of the blog.

Along with how a blog has been designed for the blogger to use, the blogger must also think of their product in terms of the user experience. Williams (2007) discusses several design characteristics that can apply to blogs. Even though his characteristics were in context of product design, a blog is a product and still needs to be thought of as a user-experience service or product. The four characteristics are physio-characteristics, socio-characteristics, ideo-characteristics and psycho-characteristics (Williams, 2007, p. 5-7). This chapter will explore the first three because they apply most to the internal design grammar of blogs.

Physio-characteristics are the physical components of a design that will affect a person. For example, when designing a blog, the blogger must think of the physical aspect of the webpage. This means they need to think of font size and color, and the width of each section of the blog. The layout of the design is just as important as the content. If it is attractive to the eyes, then the reader will be emotionally tied to it as well. We make decisions with our eyes, so we need the blog to be visually appealing (Williams, 2007; Norman, 2004). This visceral response lets us know right away if we would like to keep reading or move onto another website (Norman, 2004).

The second group, socio-characteristics, "concern[s] the ways that people relate to others and how individuals fit within social groups" (Williams, 2007, p. 6). What this means for the blogging community is that a blog can bring about a niche community who share in a similar experience (for example, mothers who have premature babies). A socio-characteristic view is how people identify themselves. For instance, mothers who have premature babies identify themselves differently than mothers with full-term babies. "A blogging community develops around these blogs to the extent that others find that they can relate their life experiences to that of the blogger or enjoy reading about his or her life events" (Price, 2010, p. 36). Blogs are a way for the community to rally behind a person.

The third characteristic, ideo-characteristics, "revolve around people's values, by what codes they try to live their lives, the conscious moral or ethical systems by which individuals make decision" (Williams, 2007, p. 7). Designers need to understand the moral and personal codes to help design products. In the case of blogs, the "aesthetic value" is key to shaping the "beauty" of the blog (Williams, 2007). The readers of the blogosphere have socially constructed what is the "right" way to design a blog. If a blog is copy-heavy, full of grammar mistakes and unorganized, it will not create a sense of community that is vital for an active discussion for a blog. It is then only a blog for the blogger and not for the community. However, if a blog is organized, grammatically correct and authentic, it has a chance to gain a following because the blog has followed the rules for creating a reputable blog.

For a blogger starting out and wanting to be successful, they must keep in mind these characteristics so they can be sure they are writing for their audience. A blogger must think of the aesthetic of the blog. Does the color and theme fit the message that I want to convey? The blogger must also think about the need of a community. If so, then there will be an audience who will read the blog if done properly. And finally, the blog needs to be well-organized, free of grammatical errors and follow the rules of the blogosphere. If these components are completed correctly, then the blogger can then begin talking to a community and gain the trust of its followers.

External Design Grammar: Developing a Community

Because the blogger only has to add content to the internal design grammar of the website, the focus of the blogger and community can be on the external design grammar of the blog, namely the development of a community that can support a friend during a health crisis. Throughout this chapter, I have mentioned how certain components of a blog support a community. With user-generated content ruling Web 2.0, there is no surprise that the number of blogs and the number of communities are increasing on the Internet. "Communication technology has expanded the options for supportive relationships" (du Pre, 2010, p. 172). The growth of blogs has fostered the growth relationships. Relationships are able to grow and be nurtured because people are able to communicate to one another at all hours of the day. Either having a shared experience with a complete stranger or wanting to understand what your friend is going through helps bring a community together around a specific blog.

Blogs can help people feel less alone (Greenberg, 2006, p. 62) since they are creating meaning through a shared experience. Morris (2010) showed that online groups offer many of the same benefits as face-to-face groups such as collaborative problem solving and sharing of information. This is a key component of the blog's purpose – to disseminate information and share experiences or ideas with others.

A blog's virtual community can be a social support system for the blogger and for the other readers. The benefit of the online community is the support system can be spread through different geographic parts of the world, but still support its members. "The readers have a shared interest in the content in the blog and therefore, feel compelled to help by writing supporting words…" (du Pre, 2010, p. 173). Because face-to-face relationships may not be feasible, online discussions can act as those personal connections and still fulfill the need of support.

Blogs also create a culture of connectivity. With blogs linking to other websites or other blogs, these hyperlinks create a sense of community and authority by providing relevant information to their audience (Funk, 2008, p. 4). "Links are the currency of the web; bloggers link to each other as a form of *quid pro quo*, sharing new content with their communities and driving traffic to each other" (Krall, 2009, p. 389). The "linkiness" of a blog helps build a community. The information sharing and commenting allows people to find relevant information quickly and easily (Scoble & Israel, 2006). "Comments and links on blogs provide evidence of a community of sharing" (Neal and McKenzie, 2011, p. 128). Being able to link to other websites or blogs provides information for the community and allows the blogger to look like an authority in the topic area (Scoble & Israel, 2006).

Neal and McKenzie (2011) studied how women with endometriosis blogged about their illness. Their findings suggest that through blogging, authors and readers were able to find informational and emotional support. The community was able to find information regarding the illness and emotional support through others because of their shared experience. The community had the illness in common. This commonality forged a community but it was through the blog where they could share their stories, experiences and information.

Malik and Coulson (2010) researched how online social support can have psychosocial benefits. Being able to talk to someone who has gone through a similar experience is so powerful because you are able to ask the questions or voice your frustrations with someone who gets it. These benefits include "improvements in coping ability, a sense of empowerment and increased psychological well-being" (Malik & Coulson, 2010, p. 141). Again, having a community who has a shared experience is crucial. It allows the community to be authentic with and support one another.

A vital piece for blogs is accessing information. Through daily posts, readers can follow a certain topic and become more familiar with what the author is experiencing. These virtual communities have similar interests and concerns and help one another access information (du Pre, 2010, p. 173). Being able to access information and share stories is an important aspect of a community, but how they receive their information is just as important. Since the community is able to read the blog in a well-organized way, the format assists in the discourse for the community. For other blogs, there is usually a comment section below each post to aid in discussion. These design features support a community and allow the community members to talk to the blogger and to one another.

A community can come together through a well-designed blog. A blog shares information and through that information creates knowledge for the followers and for the blogger. The followers provide support for the blogger and together with the blogger they create a community that trusts, shares, and supports one another.

This is exactly what CaringBridge.org does.

Case Study: CaringBridge.org

CaringBridge states its purpose as "provid[ing] free websites that connect people experiencing a significant health challenge to family and friends, making each health journey easier" ("About Us", 2011), and goes on to say that it "offers a personal and private space to communicate and show support, saving time and emotional energy when health matters most." And since the blogger websites are free to individuals, people going through a health crisis can concentrate on their own health issues and share this journey with friends and family online without having cost as an added concern.

A traditional health blog can vary in topic but it is more focused on the disease or illness and can be written by nurses, doctors or people suffering from the disease (Price, 2009; Sarasohn-Kahn, 2008). Within health blogs there is a "wisdom of crowd" mentality were people are searching for health information and the crowd (the community) is managing that wisdom together for the greater good (Sarasohn-Kahn, 2008).

Unlike a health blog, CaringBridge's focus is on the bloggers and their health journeys. It follows the blog format of being written in a diary-like commentary in reverse chronological order. It may provide information on the disease or health issue, but its primary purpose is to share updates and connect with others.

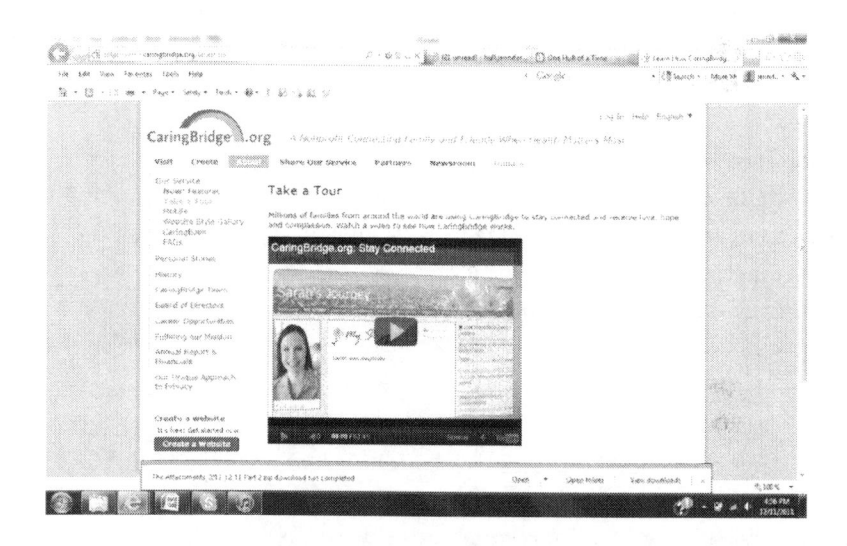

How-to video to set up a CaringBrige site, in this screenshot from www.CaringBridge.org

One community member of CaringBridge whose friend was going through a health crisis spoke about the reason why she appreciated CaringBridge's services:

> I love CaringBridge because you are able to get updates from the family without having to contact them directly. It's easy to access and get notifications via email. It's nice because you can also write

comments to the family that they can read so they know you are thinking and praying for them. I think it is also a healing process for family to write about their loved ones that are going through tough times. (Grahl, November, 17, 2011).

This easy-to-use tool both for the blogger and community member is one of the reasons why the blog is helpful. It is not cumbersome to use, which allows people to feel at ease and share their stories. This simple structure is the internal design grammar of CaringBridge. CaringBridge designed a tool that is easy-to-use and set-up, so that the blogger can quickly build an external design grammar in the community: one that can create, share, and heal.

"Research has found that a stable and supportive social network improves health outcomes for people with a wide range of conditions…" (Sarasohn-Kahn, 2008, p. 4). Having an outlet for people to share their health crisis makes the journey to healing easier. This social behavior of sharing online is a social behavior within the external design grammar of CaringBridge.

For CaringBridge, the external design grammar of the community is that it is acceptable to share online because the internal design grammar is that CaringBridge has created a safe and user-friendly place to do so.

Family members and friends can leave messages of support to their loved one, while the author is going through the health crisis. In this private, secure setting, people can share their health stories to the community and have a discussion in one webpage. It seems more personal than mass e-mailing or filling people's inboxes up with long updates or photos, and there is one central location to share a story, post pictures and develop community. Having this sense of community helps the healing process.

A design feature within CaringBridge is the Guestbook section. It is here that the community knows it is the place to write comments and well-wishes. The community can talk to the author and see what other people are writing. It provides an organized place for the community to write their comments and for the author to read them and respond. Within the internal design grammar (the Guestbook section), the external design grammar (the friends and family) can support the author who is going through the health crisis.

CaringBridge has taken the work out of setting up a personal blog and designed one for their user. The user, the author going through a health crisis, has one place where they can communicate and share their health journey. Through this easy-to-use and easy-to-read documentation, the author is able to heal through their online community's love and support.

Conclusion

Blogs gained popularity in the late 1990's and, through the lens of information design, it is easy to see why they gained popularity. Blogs are simple, well-organized and provide information to a community. Bloggers have a space to share their thoughts. For website hosts, such as CaringBridge, they provide a safe place for people going through a health crisis to share what they are going through and allow their community to follow along without the burden of phone calls, texts and e-mails. In one easy-to-use and easy-to-read place, a blogger can write about their experience and share it with others. In the eyes of the follower, the user experience is well-received since they are able to reach their goals on the blog – to access and share information with others.

References

Ancker, J., Carpenter, K., Greene, P., Hoffman, R., Kukafka, R., Marlow, L.,. . . Quillan, J. (2009). Peer-to-peer communication, cancer prevention, and the internet. *Journal of Health Communication, 14*, 38-46. doi:10.1080/10810730902806760

Blogger (2011) Retrieved November 1, 2011, from http://blogger.com

Blogpulse.com (2011) Retrieved November 17, 2011, from http://www.blogpulse.com

CaringBridge.org (2011) "CaringBridge." Retrieved October 2011, from http://www.caringbridge.org/about

Dugan, L. (2010, September 8). AP recognizes bloggers as news sources – finally. *Socialtimes.com*. Retrieved from: http://socialtimes.com/ap-recognizes-bloggers-as-news-sources-finally_b22179

du Pre, A. (2010). Communicating about health (3rd ed.), *Social support* (pp. 161-177). New York, NY: Oxford University Press.

Gee, J.P. (2003). What video games have to teach us about learning and literacy. New York, NY: Palgrave Macmillan.

Grahl, J., personal communication, November, 17, 2011

Greenberg, S. (2006, March). Building community, one mama at a time. *Off Our Backs, 36*(1), 61-62.

Funk, T. (2008). Web 2.0 and beyond – understanding the new online business models, trends, and technologies, *Power to the people* (pp. 1-31). Westport, CT: Praeger.

Jenkins, H. (2006). Convergence culture: Where old and new media collide, *Introduction: Worship at the altar of convergence* (pp. 1-24). New York, NY: New York University Press.

Krall, J. (2009). Using social metrics to evaluate the impact of online healthcare communications. *Journal of Communication in Healthcare, 2*(4), 387-394.

Kouper, I. (2010). Science blogs and public engagement with science: Practices, challenges, and opportunities. *Journal of Science Communication, 9*(1), 1-10.

Maeda, J. (2006). The laws of simplicity. Cambridge, MA: MIT Press.

Malik, S., & Coulson, N. (2010). They all supported me but I felt like I suddenly didn't belong anymore: An exploration of perceived disadvantages to online support seeking. *Journal of Psychosomatic Obstetrics & Gynecology, 31*(3), 140-149.

McKenna, L. (2007). Getting the word out: Policy bloggers use their soap box to make changes. *Review of Policy Research, 24*(3), 209-229.

Miller, E., & Pole, A. (2010). Diagnosis blog: Checking up on health blogs in the blogosphere. *American Journal of Public Health, 100*(8), 1514-1519.

Morris, H. (2008). *Premature birth and online social support: The parents' perspective* (Doctoral dissertation). Texan Woman's University, Denton, TX.

Neal, D., & McKenzie, P. (2011). Putting the pieces together: Endometriosis blogs, cognitive authority, and collaborative information behavior. *Journal of the Medical Library Association, 99*(2), 127-134. doi:10.3163/1536-5050.99.2.004

Norman, D. (2004). Emotional design, *The multiple faces of emotion and design* (pp. 35-60). New York, NY: Basic Books.

Price, B. (2010). Disseminating best practice through a web log. *Nursing Standard, 24*(29), 35-40.

Sarasohn-Kahn, J. (2008). *The wisdom of patients: Health care meets online social media*. (iHealth Reports – California HealthCare Foundation). Retrieved from California Healthcare Foundation website: http://www.chcf.org/publications/2008/04/the-wisdom-of-patients-health-care-meets-online-social-media

Scoble, R., & Israel, S. (2006). Naked conversations: How blogs are changing the way businesses talk with customers. Hoboken, New Jersey: Wiley.

Shedroff, N. (2009). Experience design 1.1. San Francisco, CA: Experience Design Books.

Williams, S. D. (2007). User experience design for technical communication: Expanding our notions of quality information design. *Proceedings of the Annual Meeting of the IEEE Professional Communication Society*.

About the Author

Jennifer L. Hull is the community coordinator for the James L. Knight School of Communication at Queens University of Charlotte. Prior to joining Queens, she worked in advertising as a media buyer for Wray Ward and then as a senior media specialist in the marketing department at Lowe's Inc. where she oversaw local advertising campaigns. She holds a B.S. in Advertising from The University of Texas at Austin and plans to receive her masters' degree in Strategic and Organizational Communication from Queens in 2013. Hull lives in Charlotte, N.C. with her husband, Brent, and their daughter, Carson.

Jennifer L. Hull

Growing with the Millennial Generation: Designing digital media for college student recruitment

Emily Carrara

The millennial generation and its integration of digital technology are actively changing the way universities and prospective students interact. Specifically, websites and social media tools such as Facebook are increasing the amount of communication universities have with prospective students. These changes are a result of the millennial generation's fluid use of technology during the quest to find the appropriate university or college and a shift in practice as colleges and universities adapt to the millennial generation's needs.

According to Tom Funk (2009) in *Web 2.0 and Beyond*, the focus of marketing falls on the needs and wants of the consumers. Today's consumers vary from those of the past because "they are increasingly sophisticated and skeptical, and increasingly active in seeking out the information, opinions, products, and services that interest them. The web is one of the principle ways that they do so" (Funk, 2009, p.1). Thus, one could discern that with the public moving towards the Internet for information as a primary research source, businesses must follow and begin to use digital technologies to reach their consumers. This is precisely the path colleges and universities have chosen in regard to their communication with prospective students. But this focus finds its roots in information design.

Saul Carliner, in *Physical, Cognitive, and Affective: A Three-part Framework for Information Design,* outlines the three models of information design and attempts to "refocus design efforts away from a preoccupation with physical design element to the potentially more fruitful exploration of the problem-solving process" (Carliner, 2000, p. 570). Using Carliner's three-part framework of information design, this chapter will explore how websites and social media tools, particularly Facebook, impact college and university recruiting processes and the reasons an emphasis on information design is necessary to successfully recruit the millennial generation and generations to come.

College and University Recruitment

Colleges and universities are held in noble regard by much of society. Their purpose is to educate young minds and to produce effective contributors to society. Receiving a college education not only is deemed respectable but also is seen as a mandatory step for achieving traditional success. And yet, like any business, a college or university must do one thing in to survive: make money.

Tuition for colleges and universities has been on the rise in recent memory. According to Christina Fierro (2010) in her article, *College tuition cost rising at a higher rate,*

> The average tuition and fees for in-state public schools over the past year increased by 7.8%... compared to an average 4.5% increase at private universities, with an average price of $27,932, according to the College Board's *Trends in College Pricing 2010 report.* (Fierro, 2010, p. 1)

Yet despite the steady increase in tuition, enrollment in colleges and universities continues to rise: "The number of full-time college students rose by 34% between 1997 and 2007, and the number of full time and part-time students increased by 3.7 million during that period" (Fierro, 2010, p.1). One could argue that this increased enrollment is driven by our economy's need for an educated workforce, or that the baby boomer generation valued college and thus their children, the millennials are attending at record setting rates despite the rising cost of tuition.

Gerard DeGroot, a professor of modern history for the University of St Andrews addressed the incoming freshman class of 2011 through an article in *The Telegraph*. He articulated that,

> Students are the true believers in education – without them, there would be no universities. Most are hungry to learn and still idealistic enough to believe that the little chunk of knowledge they acquire might make the world a better place or, at least, make them a better person. That is what you give me – a belief that progress is still possible. (DeGroot, 2011, p.1)

Idealistic or not, a university is charged with the goal of providing education to their students, but as DeGroot stated, without students, there would be no institutions of higher education. Thus, how a college or university attracts its future students is critically important and under constant reform.

The reformation required for the college or university recruitment process is necessary because with each year the constituents served by the university change on every level:

- The alumni base grows larger (former students).
- The student body loses a class through graduation (current students).
- The student body welcomes a new freshman class (future and prospective students).

The future of universities rests with prospective students being sought, directed and granted admission. Several departments typically work together to manage the recruiting process for colleges and universities. These teams are classically labeled enrollment management and are defined as: "an institution wide, systematic, comprehensive, research-driven system designed to locate, attract, and retain the students the institution wishes to serve" (Engle, 2011, p. 3).

Enrollment management teams must know the publics that they are attempting to recruit and attract to their college or university. Traditional college student recruitment has for decades been focused on glossy mailers, personal site visits by admissions counselors, and on-site campus visits. While each of these still play strongly in the admission process, today's prospective students look to technology for the information. Thus enrollment management teams must transform their recruiting strategies to remain successful and keep their institutions surviving and profiting. The need for this shift can be traced through a focus on information design.

Information Design as a Framework

Information design has been defined in a multitude of ways, its definition varying in accordance to how it is being applied. This chapter begins with a definition from Williams (2007). Information design is

> fundamentally about making information easier to understand for users, where user speed, efficiency, and accuracy – expedience- defines "easy"…and experience design embraces the complex interactions of mind, body, and emotion where the target of a product is not a "user" ripe with all the implications of that term – but instead a person, a sophisticated agent who requires entertainment, emotional satisfaction, complexity. A person respected not only for their mind, but for their body and soul, too. (Williams, 2007, p. 3)

In other words, information design is careful and thoughtful communication that occurs using all aspects of the human in mind. Or, as Saul Carliner wrote, information design is "preparing communication products so that they achieve the performance objectives established for them" (Carliner, 2000, p. 564). Thus, one can know that information design is successful when the intended message is the one the consumer receives with reverberating clarity.

To measure the level of success of information design Carliner offers the following three models of information design:

1. Physical: the ability to find information;
2. Cognitive (Intellectual): the ability to understand information; and,
3. Affective (Emotional): the ability to feel comfortable with the presentation of the information. Comfort with the information itself might not be possible, depending on the message. (Carliner, 2000, p. 564)

The physical design, based on the user's ability to find information, is a standard for how digital technology has classically communicated: an attempt at the presentation of clear concise physical data. And yet, to move away from the classic technical writing of the past, the production of information must be coupled with awareness of the effectiveness of the information on the consumer. Thus, according to Carliner's model, information design has to take into account the intellectual and emotional receptiveness of the consumer. This means understanding the users and what would appeal to them intellectually and emotionally.

Communication professor John McArthur (2011) further develops the idea of information design by including the necessity of the emotional response grounded in the user's previous experiences:

> Usability can measure quantitative affective, behavioral, and cognitive responses, but it also needs qualitative explanations to really understand the user. An individual user's experience with technology remains shaped not only by the technology she is using, but also by her past experiences with technology similar (and dissimilar) to the one being tested. (McArthur, 2011, p. 1)

McArthur moves the focus away from the presentation of the information back to the need for understanding the user and the user's history of experiences.

Thus universities need to continue to understand the students they intend to serve. And, through that lens of understanding, they can continue to improve and upgrade their digital tools to ensure that all three of Carliner's components of information design are having their intended effect on the prospective student. In the current market, this means understanding the generation enrolling in colleges today.

The Millennial Generation

The current generation that is attending or being recruited to college is one of many names: generation Y, the digital generation, the trophy generation, generation me, generation next, the net generation, the echo boomers, the now generation, the millennial generation. This millennial generation is very different from its preceding generations, generation X and the baby boomer generation.

The Generational Theory created by Neil Howe and William Strauss (1991) gave birth to the study and comparison of generations. The Generational Theory has been used to distinguish between large groups of people based on the time period they grew up in. Strauss and Howe's (1991) book *Generations: The History of America's Future, 1584 to 2069* led to this description of American generations:

> Strauss and Howe hypothesize that all of society is unfolding on a regular cyclic basis. Specifically, this cycle repeats itself every four generations (80 to 90 years) or so. They further contend that each of the four generations within each cycle has a very distinct personality. These personality types repeat, revealing apparent social similarities from one cycle to the next. (Murrary, 2011, p.1)

Strauss and Howe display a generational timeline ranging from 1433 and ending with question marks, suggesting the belief that studying generations is studying an unknown, yet cyclical, future. According to Strauss and Howe, the millennial generation is comprised of people born after 1982, and although not all experts agree, the general consensus maintains that the millennial were the last generation born in the 20th century (Murrary, 2011).

While the millennial generation has many labels, its primary unifying characteristic is the ubiquitous connection to computer technology. In the words of a member of the millennial generation, "I've grown up with this technology, and as I have grown up it has evolved, so I have been kind of learning with it" (Gibbs, 2011). This is a distinguishing characteristic because most members of the millennial generation cannot recall a time when computers did not exist.

According to the Pew Research Center in an article titled *The Millennials: Confident. Connected. Open to Change* the generation that is currently attending and being recruited by universities are on track to be "the most educated generation in American history, a trend driven largely by the demands of a modern knowledge-based economy, but most likely accelerated in recent years by the millions of 20-somethings enrolling in graduate schools, colleges or community colleges in part because they can't find a job" (2011).

According to *Millennials Bring New Attitudes*, the millennial generation will compose the majority of the workforce by 2018 (Abaffy, 2011). The Millennial generation is "generally marked by an increased use and familiarity with communications, media, and digital technologies" (Howe & Strauss,

1999, p. 6). In other words, millennials are well versed in digital communication primarily because they grew up with technology.

Marc Prensky, in *Digital Natives, Digital Immigrants (2001)*, refers to the millennial generation as "digital natives," those who have grown up with technology in their lives and thus easily speak the digital language. Older generations, or what Prensky labels "digital immigrants," are learning how to communicate with technology much like a person learns a new language; an immersion process that in lengthy and depends on the immigrant to work at learning the new language. According to Prensky, digital natives think differently than digital immigrants not only because of access to technology but because their brains have developed differently as a result of their use of technology from an early age.

In addition to being known for their unearned knowledge of technology, the millennial generation is also known for their narcissistic, egotistical, individual focus. It is from this characteristic that the labels of the trophy generation (Alsop, 2008), and generation me (Twenge, 2007) originate. Regardless of the label attributed to the millennial generation, they are a generation that will change the way we communicate, advertise, market and interact because of their ease in using digital technology to conduct all of these tasks.

With regard to institutions of higher education, the millennial generation currently comprises a large portion of the student body both at the graduate and undergraduate levels, and are the primary source of prospective students, as members of the Homeland Generation (those born after 2005) have a few years to go before being recruited by colleges and universities. To reach, engage and interact with the millennial generation and subsequent generations, colleges and universities must first learn the primary characteristics of the millennial generation.

Richard Hesel and John Pryor (2007) studied millennial students in an effort to both understand them and to give prescriptive advice on what admissions departments need to implement and change to be successful interacting with millennial students. According to Hesel and Pryor (2007, p.9) the seven defining characteristics of millennials are:

1. Conventional
2. Confident
3. Special
4. Sheltered

5. Achieving
6. Pressured
7. Team oriented

One could discern that the millennial generation believes that they are important, are pressured to attend college, and are driven to be a part of a community.

In addition to characterizing the millennial generation, Hesel and Pryor (2007) conducted a student poll where they assessed what students desire in colleges and universities. Their findings showed that:

Millenials valued:
1. National Reputation
2. Academic quality
3. Small class sizes
4. Prestige of the university
5. A close-knit campus community
6. Many opportunities for community service

Millennials did not value:
1. Specific rules about visiting hours for men/women in dorms.
2. Quality of medical and counseling services
3. The school's history and traditions
4. Emphasis on academics over career preparation
5. Friends from high school plan to attend the college

The student poll revealed that millennials still believe in the necessity and prestige associated with a collegiate education but want a very personal experience where they are more than a number in a class of hundreds of students.

Hesel and Pryor concluded their study with advice for admissions departments at colleges and universities. They advised that admissions counselors and recruiters: (1) avoid hyperbole and clichés, (2) appeal to honor and integrity, (3) demonstrate a sense of humor, (4) don't dwell on history or tradition, (5) create special web pages and other communications, (6) build connectedness, and (7) simplify complicated information (Hessel & Pryor, 2007, pp. 11-13).

The millennial generation is known for the ability to use digital technology, thus the logical connection is that admissions departments and their enrollment management committees need to engage Hessel and Pryor's advice through a move from their traditional forms of communication into the digital realm of communication.

Impact of Technology on Traditional College Recruiting Process

The traditional forms of communication used in the recruiting process of colleges and universities were predominantly books, traditional newspapers and college fairs. Books such as, *The Best 376 Colleges, The Best Colleges and Universities in the USA* or *The Complete Book of Colleges* were used to educate high school students of what was available for their future education. Yet, as the world of marketing moved to digital technology as a primary source of contact, admissions departments followed suit (Cappex.com, 2010).

For example, in 2001, President Dr. Wayne Burton of the North Shore Community College created what he called a "technological village" to develop more avenues for successful communication within all departments of the college and the community it supports. This change immensely affected the admission department, which went from collecting information on prospective students via paper "recruit cards" to using "online recruit cards" (Forsstrom, 2001, p. 28). This change increased the reaction from students from 400 cards to 4000 cards in less time and without having to increase staff. (Forsstrom, 2001). Additionally, North Shore Community College saw a "steady growth in enrollments" and "increased communication with potential applicants, timely interviews and follow ups, and increased constituent contact – all using an existing system that required no additional staffing or expense" (Forsstrom, 2001, p. 28). These findings show that making a switch from a traditional means of communication to digital communication can assist universities in increasing their level of access to potential students.

Companies such as the Princeton Review who have historically been the providers of information on the best colleges via books have moved to using websites to educate and serve their publics. The Princeton Review still markets their books on line for purchase but also provide free information for students on their website if they sign up for a membership. The site markets everything related to college admissions including prep courses for standardized tests, ranking and lists of colleges and universities, many available programs and, as a result of the website being interactive, the student can determine what categories they wish to search. Thus, one can discern that the Princeton Review has grown more effective at communicating with and educating future students (the Millennial generation) by transferring their books to interactive online websites. With the call from the millennial generation for more connection, the logical next step would be movement toward Web 2.0 technology.

Applying Information Design to College Recruiting: University Websites

At the time of their creation, computers were viewed as being similar to a task-oriented appliance. Today they have grown to become much more than an appliance; they have become what Bolter & Gromala refer to as "digital art." Instead of viewing a computer as an appliance, a tool for simple user-mediated tasks, Bolter and Gromala instead view the computer as an informational appliance that has become a form of media (radio, television, and cinema). To use their words, "It is the task of digital art to fascinate, exhilarate and sometime provoke us. Appliances on the other hand don't fascinate us, they brown our toast" (Bolter & Gromala, 2005, p. 2). Bolter and Gromala viewed the web as a medium for interaction, where the user is a part of the process.

In this world of digital art, university websites serve a multipurpose role. Primarily, a college or university website functions as the digital face of the organization. Therefore, not only must the website be visually appealing but it also must be a functional website given that it serves as an information center for prospect students. To accomplish this task, the creators of the website must create a "dynamic online environment that reflects how students think, not how the organization thinks organizationally" (Forsstrom, 2010, p. 28). In other words, college or university websites are aimed at engaging the prospective students. To be effective in doing so, they must design the site so that it caters to the needs and desires of the millennial generation.

Websites are visual representations of data entered into a computer in HTML (Hypertext Markup Language) code that are hosted on a web server. The two main categories of websites are static and interactive (IT Law Wiki, 2012). A static website is a site that is managed by a group and has a limited ability to grow. An interactive site allows for interactivity between the site owner and the site visitors in what they view. For example, an interactive website will allow users to determine their paths. In regard to prospective students using a website to gain information on a college or university, a student can choose what they are interested in or value most in their pursuit of their future academic experience by clicking on what interests them and in what order they wish. Websites that began as a static representation of data are now coming interactive sources of information.

Secondly, a college or university website often functions as the host website for the internal website used for students, staff and faculty of the college or university. This type of website is often referred to as an intranet because it can be a closed network that can only be accessed by current students, staff, and faculty of the college or university (Bradley, 2011). Utilizing this separate intranet allows the college or university webpage to serve its primary purpose of digitally displaying the university to the public, while still maintaining a separate information based or educational site for the current study body, faculty and staff.

This focused shift to presenting information for the needs of the consumer, represented earlier in the discussion on information design, lays a foundation for the movement that college recruiting is currently making in reaction to the wants and desires of the millennial generation. It is through the receptiveness of the consumer that Carliner's (2001) model becomes useful.

A university website can be effective if it adheres to Carliner's three models: physical (information is easily located by the student), cognitive (the student understands the information because it is written with the student as user in mind), and affective (the student is comfortable with the information, and thus uses it to discern next moves in the recruiting process). The ability to understand information, Carliner's cognitive model, is equally based on the user and the producer of the information. If a university creates a website it must first adhere to the physical model, and yet to have an impact on the prospective student, the information must be easily understood. Simultaneously, it must lead the prospective student toward taking action through cognitive and affective response. This action could be to apply to, contact, or simply continue to research the university.

Based on research of the millennial generation, one might presume that millennials will be most drawn to a website that shows them a school they can envision themselves attending. They want the website to be a visual representation of what they imagine college life can be like for them. Bolter and Gromala state that the "Contemporary culture is receptive not only to transparency (the window), but also an alternative, self-reflective style (the mirror) " (Bolter & Gromala, 2005, p.67). In other words, the millennial generation will be more receptive to a website that is created to serve not only as a provider of information but also as an interactive tool, allowing prospective students to reflect on their wants and desires as they research the college or university.

Given that the millennial generation craves increased interaction and connection throughout their college recruitment process (Hesel & Pryor, 2007), logic might argue that they should view their website creation through the lens of Bolter and Gromala. Colleges and universities can use the digital tool (website) as a medium for interaction between prospective students and the enrollment management team, admissions department and current students (window). Additionally, the website should be designed it in an artful way (mirror). The more appealing a website is the better the chance that a prospective student will strongly consider that particular college or university for attendance and move further in the recruiting process; which is the end goal of using technology for recruiting. Yet, even excellent websites may fall short of the needs of millenials. Through the use of Web 2.0 technology, online message boards, blogs, and interactive websites direct students toward community engagement.

Applying Information Design to College Recruiting:
Social Media (Facebook)

In addition to the use of websites, social media has been deemed a powerful and the second-most utilized tool for college recruitment (Cappex.com, 2010). The Cappex group conducted a study in 2010 in hopes of establishing a benchmark for the amount of social media enrollment management teams should use. The study generated six key findings about the increased use of social media and its positive effect on the recruiting process (see figure on page 73).

The Cappex Group found that most admissions departments use some form of social media in the admissions process. Facebook is the largest social network having grown from "7.5 million registered members at more than 2,000 U.S. colleges" (Cassidy, 2006 & Kirpatrick, 2007) to over "800 million active users today" according to the Facebook website (2012). Mark Zuckerberg, the creator of Facebook, stated that "what we are trying to do is

> 1. The use of social media in the college admission process is on the rise, though tried and true methods such as college fairs still take priority.
> 2. The social media tool that admission officers use most frequently is Facebook.
> 3. Colleges' Facebook fan pages are directed at three audiences including prospects, enrolled students and alumni, and have goals of providing campus news and answering questions.
> 4. Admission departments typically post to Facebook at least once per week.
> 5. Admission officers believe that prospective students use Facebook to get a realistic view of what a college is like.
> 6. Anecdotal evidence suggests that the biggest benefit of social media for admissions is the ability to connect with students where they are most comfortable, and the biggest drawback is the time it takes to maintain.
>
> Information from *Establishing a Benchmark for Social Media Use in College Admissions*, p. 2, Cappex.com, 2010

make it really efficient for people to communicate, get information and share information" (Locke, 2007, p.5). Zuckerberg's efforts paid off; his creation seems to be successful in both attaining and sharing information, and thus has become an effective too for businesses attempting to locate, connect and interact with their consumers.

In their 2008 article *Have you Facebooked Austin Lately? Using Technology to Increase Student Involvement,* Greg Hieberger and Ruth Harper define Facebook as, "a synthesis of many internet based communication tools previously in wide but disconnected use" (Hieberger, & Harper, 2008, p.20). The result of the synchronization of these internet tools was the attraction of millions of users. Thus, one could discern that Facebook is a valuable medium for institutions of higher education to use to increase their contact radius and build a larger community of recruitable students.

The use of Facebook also alleviates some of the communication efforts from the admissions departments and places it on current enrolled students. Through Facebook fan pages at colleges and universities, Cappex found that "prospective students us Facebook to get a realistic view of what college is like" (2010, p.7). Thus it would be logical to have students interact on the Facebook page to demonstrate to prospective students the qualities of the respective college or university.

According to Cappex, there are two primary goals for Facebook use by admissions departments. The first is to "engage students by posting relevant news and events" and the second is to "become a resource for students by monitoring wall posts and answering questions from students and parents" (2010, p. 5). These two goals connect prospective students not only to the university, but also to each other in an online community. This public and instant communication vehicle allows colleges to address many people at once. By answering one person's question on a Facebook fan page, universities can educate many viewers who read the response.

Harper and Heiberger found that "students today network with each other using technology as much as, if not more than, face-to-face communication" (Heiberger & Harper, 2008, p. 19). Thus, utilizing a Facebook fan page can allow a college or universities to engage more prospective students through a medium the millennial generation is already using.

Hieberger and Harper (2008) articulate that Facebook has continued to maintain its focus on the user experience and that "it defines itself as a company in tune with customers' experiences" (Hieberger & Harper, 2008, p.20). Facebook has been able to stay in tune with the consumer by continuing to understand and react to what its public wants from the social network. Universities using this and other online tools benefit from the consistency of upgrades to the site's information design experience, but sacrifice control over the usability of the site.

Brian Solis (2012) describes the movement that industries such as Facebook are making as changing from their original form and growing into more user-friendly forms. For the industries of higher education to become what Solis advocates, they must continue to grow externally, reaching out to more prospective students not only through university departments, but also by empowering the current students to share in the burden. A student-run Facebook page has the ability to hold more credibility in describing life as a college student then any page run by administrators. This credibility is different because it is based on the needs and wants of the millennial generation, not the needs and wants of the University. One could discern that Solis's concept of 'Consumer Revolution' is coming to fruition with regard to college recruiting (Solis, 2012).

Concluding Statement

Digital technology has broadened the scope of traditional college recruiting. This has allowed the recruiting process to grow from local roots and move to working nationally. Thus, technology has awarded colleges and universities more access to potential students. The burden now rests on how colleges and technologies will utilize this technology. If they fulfill Carliner's (2000) three-part approach, create and update their websites, and create Facebook pages with the wants and needs of the millennial generation in mind, information design and technology can together improve the college recruiting process and draw more students into universities. In other words, the use of digital technology is enlarging the community of potential students for colleges and universities.

This chapter has explored how websites and social media tools, specifically Facebook, are enlarging the recruitable community for colleges and universities. How this technology is used to design information determines its effectiveness. In the implementation and creation of websites and Facebook pages, it is necessary that college and universities adhere to Carliner's three step framework and also take time to understand the wants and needs of their potential students, the millennial generation and subsequent generations to follow. Using this user-focused model, colleges and universities will be able to communicate with prospective students on multiple levels and through multiple avenues of communication. The use of social media empowers the credibility of the portrayal of college life presented by the admissions department because it uses the narratives of current students. Moreover, social media also serve to connect prospective students with current students.

Although changes can be difficult to make, it is in the best interest of colleges and universities to move towards digital forms of communication in their recruiting process. "Colleges and universities are not built to change. In many ways they are built to resist change. This preservation of the status quo could represent the single greatest threat to survival and success in the future" (Crockett & Engle, 2011, p. 17). Thus, this chapter advocates for increased focus on user-experience in the use of digital technology by colleges and universities. With that focus, institutions of higher education can recruit students and continue to educate the millennial generation, and the generations to come.

References and Further Resources

Abaffy. L. (2011). Millennials bring new attitudes. ENR.com online publication. Retrieved from http://enr.construction.com/business_management/workforce/2011/0223newattitudes-1.asp

Barwell, G., Moore C., & Walker, R., Marking machinima: A case study in assessing student use of a web 2.0 technology. *Australasian Journal of Educational Technology 27*(5), 765-780. Retrieved from http://www.ascilite.org.au/ajet/ajet27/ajet27.html.

Bucknell University (2011). Bucknell University Web Site. Retrieved from http://www.bucknell.edu

Bradley, M., (2011) Intranet. About.com. Retrieved from http://compnetworking.about.com/cs/intranets/g/bldef_intranet

Cappex.com (2010).Establishing a Benchmark for Social Media Use in College Admissions: 2010 Social Media and College Admissions Study. Retrieved from http://www.cappex.com/media/EstablishingABenchmarkForSocialMediaUse.pdf

Carliner, S. (2000). Physical, cognitive, & affective: A three-part framework for information design. *Technical Communication.* 561-576.

Cassidy, J. (2006). Me media. New Yorker. 50-59.

Ching, Y., & Hsu, Y. (2011). Design-grounded assessment: A framework and a case study of web 2.0 practices in higher education. *Australasian Journal of Educational Technology.* 781-797.

Crockett, D., & Engle, C. (2011). Ten things you need to know to jump start your enrollment management committee. Retrieved from http://www.dixie.edu/reg/SEM/Engel.pdf

DeGroot, G., (2011). University there's no better place to be at 18. *The Telegraph.* Retrieved from http://www.telegraph.co.uk/education/universityeducation/studentlife/8781988/Universitytheres-no-better-place-to-be-at-the-age-of-18.html.

Facebook. (2012) Facebook Website Statistics. Retrieved from http://www.facebook.com/press/info.php?statistics

Faculty Focus. (2009). Twitter in Higher Education: Usage Habits and Trends of Today's College Faculty. Retrieved from http://www.scribd.com/doc/19253028

Fierro, C. (2010). College tuition cost rising at a higher rate. Retrieved from http://www.dailyfinance.com/2010/10/28/college-tuition-costs-rising-at-a-higher-rate/

Forsstrom, J. (2008). Technology streamlines and improves recruitment—and institutional performances. *New England Journal of Higher Education, 23*(1), 28.

Funk, T. (2009). Web 2.0 and Beyond: understanding the new online business models, trends, and technologies. Library of Congress Cataloging-in-publication Data.

Gibbs, A. (2011). Interview with Emily Carrara Notes. Interview conducted on 11/12/2011 at Queens University of Charlotte Campus.

Gillford, J. (2010). Digital public relations: E-marketing's big secret. *Continuing Higher Education Review, 74*, 62-72.

Harpel-Burke, P. (2006). Medium-sized universities connect to their libraries: Links on university home pages and user groups pages. *Information Technology and Libraries, 25*(1), 12-23.

Harris, K. (2008). Using Social Networking Sites as Student Engagement Tools. *Diverse Issue in Higher Education , 25* (18), 40.

Heiberger, G., & Harper, R. (2008). Have You Facebooked Austin Lately? Using Technology to Increase Student Involvement. *New Directions for Student Services*, 124, 19-35.

IT Law Wiki, Wikia Lifestyle. (2012) Wikia.com. Retrieved from http://itlaw.wikia.com/wiki/Interactive_website

Junco, R., & Cole-Avent, G. A. (2008). An Introduction to Technologies Commonly Used by College Students. *New Directions for Student Services 124*, 3-17.

Kang, S., & Norton, H. (2006). Colleges and universities use of the world wide web: A public relations tool for school excellence in the digital age. Conference Papers—International Communication Association, 1-30.

Kirkpatrick, D. (2007). Facebook's plan to hook up the world. *Fortune, 155*(11), 127.

Locke, L. (2007, July 17). The future of Facebook. *Time Magazine*. Retrieved from
http://www.time.com/time/business/article/0,8599,1644040,00

Mattson, E., & Barnes, N. G. (2009). Social Media and College Admissions: The First Longitudinal Study. University of Massachusetts Dartmouth. Retrieved from http://www.umassd.edu/cmr/studiesresearch/mediaandadmissions.cfm

Martinez, A., Wartman, A., & Lynk, K. (2009). *Online social networking on campus: understanding what matters in student culture.* New York: Rutledge.

McArthur, J. (2011) Usability + Design = User Experience . JAMcAthur.com Retrieved from http://jamcarthur.com/2011/06/20/usability-design-user-experience/

Murrary, W. (2011). Introduction. The Time Page. Retrieved from http://www.timepage.org/time.html

Nealy, M. J. (2009). The New Rules of Engagement. *Diverse Issues in Higher Education, 26* (3), 13.

Neibling, J. (2010). Speaking the language of today's digital natives. *Community College Journal, 81*(1), 14-15.

Peluchette, J., & Karl, K. (2010). Examining Students' Intended Image on Facebook: "What Were They Thinking?" *Journal of Education for Business , 85* (1), 30-37.

Pulley, J. (2010). In full bloom. *Currents, 36*(2), 16-21.

Prensky, M. Digital natives digital immigrants. *On The Horizon,* 9(5), 1-6.

Princeton Review Website (2011). Retrieved from http://www.princetonreview.com.

Princeton Review (2012). *The best 376 colleges 2012 edition (college admissions guide).* MA: 2011 Princeton Review INC.

Princeton Review (2011). *The complete book of colleges, 2012 edition (college admissions guide).* MA: Princeton Review INC.

Strauss, W., & Howe, N., (1991). *Generations.* New York: William Morrow Publisher.

Tillotson, J. (2002) Web site evaluation: A survey of undergraduates. *Online Information Review, 26* (6),392-403 Retrieved from http://www.emeraldinsight.com/journals.htm?articleid=862200&show=html

The best colleges and universities in the USA. Abe Books INC. www.abebooks.com

Tucciarone, K. M. (2009). Speaking the Same Language: Information College Seekers Look for on a College Web Site. *College & University, 84* (4), 22-31.

Violino, B. (2009). The Buzz on Campus: Social Networking Takes Hold. *Community College Journal, 79*(6), 28-30

Wandel, T. (2008). Colleges and Universities Want to be Your Friend: Communicating via Online Social Networking. *Planning for Higher Education, 37*(1), 35-48.

Wright, J. (2010). A quick flick through Facebook. *Evaluation & Research in Education,* 70-73.

About the Author

Emily Carrara, originally from Corrales, New Mexico, attended Winthrop University on a volleyball scholarship. Carrara graduated with honors, earning a Bachelor's of Arts Degree in Political Science with dual minors in Spanish and Social Sciences, in May of 2007. Carrara is the current Assistant Volleyball coach for Queens University of Charlotte where she is pursuing her Master's Degree in Communication. As a vibrant member of the Queens community, Carrara also serves as an ACE mentor, the assistant coaches' liaison, and the staff advisor for both the Toms Club and Ping Pong Club on campus. Carrara currently resides in Charlotte, North Carolina with her husband Chris.

Emily Carrara

Designing Online Credibility:
Bloggers as leaders in audience and expertise

Kenyon Stanley

In Spring 2011, governments all over the Middle East began to topple. Several leaders found themselves unable to control their people. According to the Arab Spring archived files at Cornell University (2011), on January 27, 2011 hundreds of thousands of Egyptian protesters gathered in Cairo and Alexandria calling for "an end to corruption, injustice, poor economic conditions and an end in the thirty-year regime of President Hosni Mubarak" (p. 1). Many of the leaders tried to silence the crowds through censorship and in some cases violence. One demonstrator known as Blogging Egypt (2011) wrote, "Security forces hosed protesters with water and shot tear gas into the crowds" (p. 6). However, the people stood strong and sixteen days after the protesters first gathered, President Mubarak resigned.

The Arab Spring archived files at Cornell (2011) continue to document that two days after the protesters first gathered, the Egyptian government shut down the Internet and cellular phone service. However, the protesters still gathered, blogs were written and the Egyptian regime was ultimately dismantled. Bloggers can influence communities (for good or ill). Blogging is a tool that, when used appropriately, individuals can use to influence audiences by creating communities and communicating credible information. Anyone equipped with a computer and internet access has the ability to send and receive messages to or from practically anywhere in the world. The rapid flow of information has given individuals the power to speak to communities and influence decision makers.

This chapter will discuss the history of blogging, current trends in blogging and the status of blogs as recognized by the Associated Press and other information outlets. Next, the chapter will explore the subject of credibility, specifically author credibility, and how credibility is established in both traditional and online environments. Lastly, this chapter will explain how information design connects to the credibility of blogs by describing specific strategies that bloggers can employ to contribute to the conversation.

History of the Blog

According to Byron and Broback (2006), the term "weblog" was coined in 1997 by early American blogger Jorn Barger. Later shortened to "blog," the term and blog usage didn't gain popularity until 2000. Early bloggers used these websites primarily to discuss areas of personal interest and web-browsing habits. By 2004, the term blog was Merriam-Webster Dictionary's word of the year.

According to BlogPulse (2011), just over 152 million blogs existed in 2010. Byron & Broback (2006) divide the blogosphere into major categories of blogs including personal blogs, company blogs, and brand blogs. Personal blogs document a blogger's personal experiences. Company or corporate blogs communicate core values or strategic goals of an organization. Brand blogs are often marketing tools that seek to enhance brand awareness or brand identity through open dialogue in an online environment.

Today, blogs receive coverage in major newspapers and businesses are beginning to realize the importance of the blog. One example of the growing impact of blogging on business occurred in 2010 when so-called "mommy bloggers" took on a brand in their blogs. According to Skepys (2010), hundreds of angry mothers began attacking a new Pampers diaper in 2010. Complaining that the diaper didn't work and caused severe rashes, mothers all across the nation began to voice their concerns and stories in the world of blogs (termed the blogosphere). Skepys continues to explain that, when the story was broadcast on CNN , Pampers realized that they were in a brand reputation crisis. Within 48 hours, Pampers took the necessary steps to end the firestorm. Pampers realized that the concerned parents had credibility amongst their growing audience and recognized that to secure the company's brand reputation, Pampers needed to change the narrative of the story that was speeding out of control (for more information about Pampers and the Mommy Blogger crisis, see Skepys' 2010 article on socialmediainfluence.com). By reacting quickly and utilizing an integrated media approach, Pampers was able to change the message and quickly restore their market share.

Thus, personal blogs, like those of the mommy bloggers, have not only influenced business, but have also begun to influence journalism and media coverage. As individuals witness newsworthy events, people document their accounts of such events on blogs.

According to Garden (2010), the preexisting barriers between passive audience and objective journalist have been broken by the rise of the blog. Bloggers are reporting and their communities are reading and responding to the authors on many levels. Readers can comment, send the blog post to other social platforms, and become part of the story instead of simply passively reacting to how mainstream media frames the story.

This sudden shift in journalism hasn't gone unnoticed by mainstream media. According to Byron & Broback (2006), bloggers have gained credibility in traditional media outlets and most news agencies now refer to blogs while developing their stories, a notion that media professionals would have balked at a few years earlier. According to Fisher (2010), the Associated Press (AP) had a history of downplaying the role of blogs in news reporting. However in September of 2010, the AP addressed its members and officially announced that the AP would begin to recognize blogs as credible news sources. This issue of credibility has remained one of fundamental importance to bloggers as they develop audience and expertise in an online environment.

Credibility

When Aristotle laid out the three pillars of persuasion, ethos, pathos, and logos, he suggested that each could inspire an audience to shift its thinking. Ethos is often rephrased as credibility in contemporary communication. According to Craig (2010), "Ethos is the principle that in order to be effective, you must be credible and must continually reinforce that credibility by your thoughts, words and deeds" (p. 55).

Communication scholar Julia Wood (2011) notes that credibility occurs "when listeners believe a speaker and trust what the speaker is saying" (p. 276). Credibility is not found in the person himself, but is found in the perceptions of his audience. Wood continues to say that credibility can be based on the audience's perceptions of the speaker's "position, authority, knowledge (also called expertise), dynamism and trustworthiness (also called character)" (p. 276). Additionally, Wood (2011) suggests that credibility can be broken down into three distinct categories: initial credibility, derived credibility and terminal credibility.

Initial credibility is the expertise, dynamism and character that readers attribute to speakers before they begin to speak, or before authors begin to write (Wood, 2011). An example of initial credibility might occur when a college professor addresses his first class of the term. Although many students may have not read the text for the course, the professor's education, job title, and experience would give the class (audience) a sense of trust that the professor has expertise and knowledge in the field the students desire to learn. Likewise, a blogger could have initial credibility if she is an expert in her subject matter, has written previous articles or books, or has established a name for herself with an audience.

Derived credibility occurs during the actual process of communicating (Wood, 2011). It can relate to the flow of communication, its clarity, and its organization. A speaker might achieve derived credibility from the dynamism she exhibits on stage or from the audience members' feelings of engagement during the speech. Derived credibility can also relate to the sources and experts a speaker chooses to reference. Credible sources add credibility to a speaker who cites them. A blogger might achieve derived credibility by writing blog posts that are engaging, clear and well-organized or that contain convincing evidence that support whatever claim the author is making.

Terminal credibility "is the cumulative combination of initial and derived credibility" (Wood, 2011, p. 276). It is the perception of credibility that a speaker attains in his audience when the speech concludes. A blogger could achieve terminal credibility when she has built an audience over time that recognizes the author as a valuable source of information that is communicated in an honest and thought provoking way.

Cornell University Library (2011) advises students to check the credibility of authors in specific ways. First, a reader should check the author's credentials. Is the author an expert in the subject he/she is writing about? Does the author have advanced education in the subject? What is the author's experience? These questions point toward an author's initial credibility. Second, a reader should objectively look at the evidence being provided. This means that the reader should critically evaluate all of the evidence that the author uses to support his claim and question the credibility of each source. Many bloggers link their sources within their blog posts. Additionally, many bloggers establish credibility through pictures and videos. For example, a blogger who witnesses a breaking news story could enhance her credibility by taking pictures or shooting video of the event and including them in the blog. These issues of source credibility point toward derived credibility, and when combined with initial credibility, can help an blogger achieve terminal credibility.

In an online environment, "people sometimes carefully analyze the information and its features, and at other times they use a more holistic and intuitive approach based on their feelings and at other times they may draw upon their other people in their social circle" (Metzger, et.al., 2011, p. 4). Depending on the context, researchers suggest that people will employ either analytical, heuristic or social approaches when evaluating credibility of a message. An analytic approach to evaluating credibility occurs while the reader is carefully analyzing the information and all of its features. In contrast, A heuristic method of analyzing credibility occurs when a reader draws upon his feelings, intuition or other holistic methods in order to discern credibility in a message. Lastly, a group-based method of analyzing credibility occurs when the reader draws upon other people in her social circle for advice and guidance regarding the credibility of a message.

Furthermore, Pure et. al. (2011) explains that the proliferation of experience-driven content such as user-generated ratings, reviews and testimonials has transformed the notion of expertise to competence. This means that the influence of credentialed expertise has been diminished as more and more people are contributing to online dialogues.

In an online environment, a reader must look at whether or not the information being delivered is a primary or secondary source of information. Pure et. al. (2011) states that primary sources of online information and secondary sources of information are used mutually while ascertaining the credibility of a message. Primary sources of information are those in which the audience places trust above other sources whereas secondary sources are tools used to evaluate the credibility of a primary source. For example, a blog reader may analyze reader comments (secondary source) as she is determining whether or not a blog post (primary source) is credible.

Pure et. al. (2011) continues to explain that people grant cognitive authority to sources that describe personal experience in a different way than they would grant authority to the presentation of facts. A good example of this concept can be found in social support blogs. According to Neal and

McKenzie, (2011), "While peer support tools such as health blogs may not meet librarians' traditional standards for authority, they might provide both the social support and the affectively authoritative and situationally relevant information that information seekers value" (p. 133). Cancer survivors may enjoy the dialogue that they would find in a survivor support group and learn from personal experiences. However, someone suffering from cancer may want to find information on alternative methods to cancer treatment to become informed on all of the available options.

Macario, Ednacot, Ullberg, and Reichel (2011) report that "over 80% of US consumers are seeking health information online" (p. 145), but the credibility of the information found depends on the type of information desired by the reader. Therefore, credibility in the blogosphere is related to both the author and the intent of the reader.

Information Design and Blogs

A natural next step for this chapter is to try to discern how a blogger might develop credibility through a blog. To begin this conversation, the chapter turns to the field of information design. According to experience designer and author Nathan Shedroff, "Information design has only recently been identified as a discipline; it is one in which we all participate and, in some way, we always have" (2009, p. 34). Shedroff (2009), continues to say that information design is "a continuum from data, a somewhat raw ingredient, to wisdom, an ultimate achievement" (p.3 4). In essence, information design is the experience from data analysis to wisdom the reader undergoes while discerning a message.

Shedroff continues, "We have learned from information design that structure, itself, has meaning and that it can affect not only the effectiveness but the meaning of the message" (2009, p. 34). This means that the design or structure of a message/information is more than data. In fact, the design of a message provokes reactions with the reader that can enhance or even change the meaning of a text. Think about a manager's office. Typically, it would include a desk, some chairs, maybe a bookshelf. How that office is arranged can drastically change perceptions of the space. According to Knapp and Hall (2006), "U.S. office buildings are constructed from a standard plan that reflects a pyramidal organization" (124). In a manager's office, there will typically be a desk between the superior and subordinate. The desk is a barrier that highlights the power distance between subordinate and superior. When the boss calls a subordinate into her/his office, the proxemics of the space can affect the meaning of the message. Just as the structure of an office has the ability to affect the meaning of a message, the structure of an online forum does as well.

Shedroff (2006) explains that "most design works on many levels that the viewer, participant, or user isn't even aware of throughout the experience" (p. 74). One example of this concept can be found in the popular furniture store IKEA. At first glance, the store appears to be a massive building where customers can find furniture or other household items. However, each area of IKEA stores are strategically designed to give the customer a unique shopping experience where shoppers are directed through all the items in the store. They can find what they need and wonder about what they could have at the same time. Like the IKEA store, a blog is both a warehouse of information and an experience for both the reader.

Kress, G. and Van Leeuwen, T. (2001), suggest new "grammars" for other semiotic modes. Similar to language, these "new" grammars can be socially created and contain varying sets of available changing resources for making meaning. This means that new grammars contain continually fluctuating components that contribute to the meaning of the message. For example, a blog contains reader comments that the entire audience is able to view. In some cases, the original author will respond to reader comments. Whether the comments (both reader and author) are intended to change, reify or compliment the original meaning of the text, the fact remains that reader/author dialogue affects the message making process.

Kress & Van Leeuen (2001), continue to state that the aural and visual techniques have received precise attention over other modal forms. However, Accounting for multimodality is considered a very important ongoing project, given the importance of the visual mode in contemporary communication. Multimodality is simply the communication that occurs in and across a full range of semiotic modes (e.g. verbal, visual, and aural). This means that what we see and what we hear is only part of the message. How a message affects us entirely constitutes the experience users feel during the process.

Bloggers should also understand the human characteristics that their blog touch on their readers. According to Williams (2007), "good designs communicate on multiple layers, that involve the multiple channels people use to assign meaning" (p. 5). Williams (2006) continues by identifying the following traits as human characteristics affected by design: physio-characteristics, socio-characteristics, ideo-characteristics and psycho-characteristics.

Physio-characteristics "concern the physical bodies of people, the way that we use our bodies and how our bodies exist in physical environments" (Williams, 2007, p. 5). For a blog, the most important physio-characteristics could involve ensuring that the blog is readable to an audience that may have a physical handicap (e.g. blindness or deafness). Conversely, the physio-characteristic of a reader could involve special abilities that some of the audience may have (e.g. the ability to understand hashtags and text type).

Williams (2007) states that socio-characteristics "concern the ways that people relate to others and how individuals fit within social groups" (p. 5). The socio-characteristics of a blog could include the culture of the audience and author. The author might consider if the audience is local, regional, global, or industry-specific. By understanding the demographics of an audience, a blogger is better able to speak directly to them. For example, if a blogger is writing to a global audience, he might omit metaphors primarily used in the United States or write outside the boundaries of a Eurocentric framework.

Ideo-characteristics "revolve around people's values, by what codes they try to live their lives, the conscious moral or ethical systems by which individuals make decisions" (Williams, 2007, p. 6). The ideo-characteristics of a blog would involve the value systems and moral codes of the audience and author. This would include religious beliefs, aesthetic values, and personal and social ideologies. Ideo-characteristics are probably the most complex traits to comprehend in a global blogosphere, unless the author is writing to a specific audience that embodies a specific set of values.

Finally, psycho-characteristics "reveal individual talents, skills or traits, ones that do not necessarily concern a person's relationships to others" (Williams, 2007, p.6). The psycho-characteristics of a blog would include any special skills or techniques of the audience and author. Psycho-characteristics might reveal themselves primarily in industry specific blog sites. For example, a structural engineering firm may subscribe to a blog site that contains unique jargon that a non-trained person may not comprehend. By understanding and incorporating these human characteristics into a blog, the blogger might have a better chance to reach and connect with a targeted and large audience.

Developing credibility through blog design

Previously this chapter discussed how blogs have gained momentum over the last two decades and information about the establishment of credibility online. Furthermore, this chapter has provided bloggers with several helpful information design topics that could enhance and transform a blog into an interactive experience that can be enjoyed by the author and reader. The next section of this chapter will discuss how information design can impact credibility and engage a community.

Designing initial credibility

Whether a blogger wants to report on breaking news, write about the joys and challenges of parenthood, share experiences about struggling with a life-changing disease or effectively communicate with others during a national disaster, a well-designed blog can generate an audience that uses the blog by reading and sharing information with others. According to Solis, B. (2011), "The blog is your hub for demonstrating expertise, sharing vision, listening to and responding to customers, communicating progress, curating relevant market and trend information and hosting dialogues" (p. 27). This means that an effective and successful blog will be a good host for a conversation.

To be a good host, an author needs initial credibility. As previously stated, initial credibility, might be attained by having a particular credential, being a published author, or developing a unique point of view. In the blogosphere, blogging can be a "springboard for a multi-platform delivery tool" (Norrington, 2010, p. 97). Successful bloggers can develop initial credibility by engaging their prospective audiences through multiple channels like Twitter, Facebook, or YouTube in addition to the blog. Linking a blog to other social networking platforms increases the potential for a blog to engage a larger audience.

Norrington (2010) also suggests some other practices that might give a blog credibility. First, bloggers need to develop unique, interesting and relevant avatars. An avatar is a computer-generated character that readers see when they read the blog. Some bloggers choose to use their own picture while others create a character from scratch. There are benefits to both. An actual picture gives the blog authenticity since the readers actually see the face of the author.

Norrington (2010) also advises that bloggers limit the length of their blogs to no more than 500 words. The reason is that readers do not read on their computers is the same way that they read novels. Blog readers have short attention spans. Therefore bloggers need to be able to deliver their message clearly and concisely.

Lastly, Norrington (2010) advises bloggers to give their readers a call-to-action. One effective way to call your readers to action is to offer a reward to encourage meaningful interaction. For example, some blogs might offer gift cards for the comment that gets the most positive response. In offering a reward for comments, readers are not only reading the original blog, but they are reading the comments of others and perhaps engaging in meaningful dialogue with other readers as well.

Designing derived credibility

According to Petterson (2010), the design of digital content focuses on three specific areas: structure, levels, and hierarchy. First, a designer must develop a clear structure for the content to be included in a blog post. This means that information should flow. In the blogosphere, readers want to experience the words, not just read them. Bloggers are sharing their experiences with an audience. If the structure of the blog is disheveled or choppy, the reader most likely won't give the author the derived credibility necessary to successfully engage in a co-created experience.

This concept of structure has a technology component as well. According to Gerken, et. al. (2009), "it is essential that the system provide different ways of formulating such an information need, depending on the kind of information the user already has." (p. 51). Bloggers should be aware of the different methods their readers may use to access the blog. For example, in the last 5 years, the technology surrounding smart phones has significantly evolved. People can now access web sites, blogs and nearly all social media platforms from their phone. The screen size is smaller on a phone and a lot of the graphics that would normally appear on a desktop computer may not be accessible on a phone. Most blogging platforms have built-in capacity for bloggers to ensure that smart phone readers can access the blog. Ensuring that the blog settings are smart phone friendly greatly enhances the structure of the blog.

Petterson's second area of focus, levels, suggests that designers need to limit the number of levels in the structure. For bloggers, structural levels could pertain to the content itself. Most successful bloggers have a specific niche and stick to it. By doing so, a blogger can establish derived credibility over time with an audience that shares a common interest.

Third, Petterson submits that designers should "show the hierarchy structure of the content in the graphic design" (p.172). This demonstration could take shape in the graphics, pictures, images or tag lines in a blog. For example, if the blog author compliments her text with pictures or videos that are consistent with the message, or that detail actual events, then the reader is receiving consistent messages while using different senses. Reading a blog is like any other message decoding process—it is an experience. By designing a blog that effectively communicates to the reader visually, aurally and verbally, the reader will receive an enriching experience that will ultimately enhance the author's credibility.

Developing terminal credibility

Successful blogs are interactive sites that give readers and authors the opportunity to engage in dialogue. When the discussion is one of mutual interest, the dialogue becomes meaningful. As the dialogue continues, initial, derived and terminal credibility are achieved and strengthened through mutual understanding. As long as the information that is being shared is true, it stands to reason that credibility will strengthen over time.

As previously discussed, developing terminal credibility occurs when initial and derived credibility have been successfully applied. This can be difficult for a blog. For example as Pure et al. (2011) explains that the influence of credentialed expertise has been diminished as more and more people are contributing to online dialogues. Pure et al. (2011) continues to explain that audiences judge the credibility of a message by attributing elements of the message to a primary or secondary source of information. For a blog and other online documents, the reader determines credibility through research. Today's readers have the luxury to go to the primary source of information at any time. So, truth and trustworthiness can be established relative to other sources.

Additionally, an author that responds to reader comments and acknowledges the reader's role in the process changes the transfer of information from a one-way, asymmetrical exchange to a two-way, symmetrical dialogue. Therefore, readers who may be confused about a particular point of the message realize that they can go to either the author or external sources for clarification.

Good information design and credibility are mutually inclusive notions. In fact, effective information design can contribute to a blogger's initial and derived credibility. For example, if a blog post is well written, aesthetically pleasing and relevant to the genre of the message, then the reader will not be confused or overloaded with mixed-messages. The attainment of initial and derived credibility will lead to terminal credibility amongst the audience.

Conclusion

This chapter has discussed the history of the blog and how it has transformed from a one-way information dissemination tool to a multi-user information sending and receiving system. Furthermore, reading and writing blogs has gained popularity amongst professionals and amateurs. With the mass-influx of information, the question of credibility has come up. Today, there are over 152 million blogs that discuss everything from personal experiences to company or brand information. Furthermore, the AP has recently recognized blogs as credible sources for journalists to reference. Today, nearly every news agency refer to blogs during the creation of a story. With so many blogs in the blogosphere, design has become an important part of the message making process of blogs.

Information design is the experience both reader and author take on while decoding a message—in this case blogs. Blogs are not simply text on a computer screen. In fact, the design of the blog contributes just as much, if not more to the message making process. Furthermore, this chapter has discussed the importance of reaching the audience's on physio-, psycho-, socio- and ideo- levels while crafting a message. A successful blog will connect with the reader on all of those levels.

This chapter also discussed the role of credibility in a blog. Blog authors today have a unique opportunity to craft messages that give their readers an experience. It's not just the text. In fact, the design of the blog can either enhance the meaning of the words or change the meaning altogether. To be credible, blog authors must engage their audiences on multiple levels and allow for the two-way discourse to become meaningful to the reader. Data is everywhere in the world. However, the data we consider meaningful will stick with us.

References

Arab Spring Library Guide (2011). Library guide at Cornell University. http://guides.library.cornell.edu/content.php?pid=259276&sid=2159613

Benbasat, I., & Taylor, R. N. (1978). The Impact of Cognitive Styles on Information System Design. *MIS Quarterly, 2*(2), 43-54.

Blogging Egypt (2011). My social and political commentary on the world- from Egypt to Italy and beyond. Retrieved, January 7, 2012, from http://wayback.archiveit.org/2358/20110201013235/http://blogginegegypt.blogspot.com/

Cornell University Library. (2011). *Critically analyzing information sources.* http://olinuris.library.cornell.edu/ref/research/skill26.htm.

Craig, H. (2010). Aristotle teaches project management. *Contractor Magazine, 57*(6), 47-56.

Droge, C., Stanko, M. A., & Pollitte, W. A. (2010). Lead Users and Early Adopters on the Web: The Role of New Technology Product Blogs. *Journal Of Product Innovation Management, 27*(1), 66-82.

Fisher, L. (2010). AP begins crediting bloggers as news sources. *TNW Social Media.* 7, September, 2010. http://thenextweb.com/socialmedia/2010/09/07/ap-begins-crediting-bloggers-as-news-sources/.

Garden, M. (2010). Newspaper Blogs: The genuine article or poor counterfeits? *Media International Australia* (135), 19-31.

Gerken, J., Heilig, M., Jetter, H., Rexhausen, S., Demarmels, M., König, W., & Reiterer, H. (2009). Lessons learned from the design and evaluation of visual information-seeking systems. *International Journal on Digital Libraries, 10*(2/3), 49-66.

Knapp, M. L., & Hall, J. (2006). *Nonverbal communication in human interaction.* Belmont, CA: Thompson/Wadsworth.

Kress, G. and Van Leeuwen, T. (2001) *Multimodal Discourse: The Modes and Media of Contemporary Communication Discourse.* London: Arnold.

Macario, E., Ednacot, E., Ullberg, L., & Reichel, J. (2011). The changing face and rapid pace of public health communication. *Journal of Communication in Healthcare, 4*(2), 145-150.

Metzger, M. J., Flanagin, A. J., Medders, R., Pure, R. A., Hartsell, E., & Markov, A. (2011). An Investigation of Youth and Digital Information Credibility. Paper presented at the National

Communication Association (NCA) Annual Conference, New Orleans, LA.

Neal, D. M., & McKenzie, P. J. (2011). Putting the pieces together: endometriosis blogs, cognitive authority, and collaborative information behavior. *Journal of The Medical Library Association, 99*(2), 127-134.

Norrington, A. (2010). Harnessing 'e' in Storyworlds: Engage, Enhance, Experience, Entertain. *Publishing Research Quarterly, 26*(2), 96-105.

Pettersson, R. (2010). Information Design--Principles and Guidelines. *Journal of Visual Literacy, 29*(2), 167-182.

Pure, R. A., Westcott-Baker, A., Metzger, M. J., & Flanagin, A. J. (2011). Credibility in a social media environment. Paper presented at the National Communication Association (NCA) Annual Conference, New Orleans, LA.

Ransbotham, S., & Kane, G. C. (2011). Membership turnover and collaboration success in online communities: Explaining rises and falls from grace in wikipedia. *MIS Quarterly, 35*(3), 613-627.

Royal Pingdom. (2011). *Ramblings from the pingdom team about the internet and webtech.* 1/27/11/. http://wayback.archive-it.org/2358/20110201013235/http://bloggingegypt.blogspot.com/

Shedroff, N. (2009) *Experience Design 1.1.* 6th Edition. Shedroff.

Skepys, B. (2010). Pampers takes on mommy bloggers and wins. *Social Media Influence.* http://socialmediainfluence.com/2010/05/10/pampers-takes-on-mommy-bloggers-and-wins/.

Solis, B. (2011). *Engage.* 2nd Edition. Wiley & Sons: Hoboken, N.J.

Williams, S.D. (2007). User Experience Design for Technical Communication:
Expanding Our Notions of Quality Information Design. *Conference Papers--*

Winter, S., Krämer, N., Schielke, K., & Appel, J. (2010). Credibility in the Blogosphere: Source Effects on the Selection of Online Science Information. *Conference Papers -- International Communication Association,* 1.

Wood, J. (2011) *Communication Mosaics.* 6th ed. Boston, Ma: Wadsworth.

About the Author

Kenyon Stanley has been a nonprofit executive for over 10 years. Currently, Stanley consults for various nonprofit and for-profit agencies in social and new media strategies, and is a graduate student in the Master of Arts in Organizational and Strategic Communication in the James L. Knight School of Communication at Queens University of Charlotte.

Kenyon Stanley

QR Codes:
Click, snap, save to erase the digital divide

Davida Jackson

In 2000, U.S. President Bill Clinton addressed the issue of communication technology disparities for the first time to the American people in a 'National Call To Action': "Our mission is to open the digital frontier to all Americans, regardless of income, education, geography, disability or race...If we work together to close the digital divide, technology can be the greatest equalizing force our society or any other has ever known." This national call to action challenged big corporations and non-profits to bridge the digital divide.

Generally speaking, the term 'digital divide' refers to inequality in the knowledge of or use of new communication technologies (Gilbert, 2010). According to the Pew Internet & American Life project (2011), during the year of President Clinton's speech, less than half of the nation had access to the Internet. The same study shows that while Internet adoption grew since that time, the ways individuals connect to the online world have also changed. Now, many people are surfing the World Wide Web using smart phones.

First, this chapter will explore the digital divide from a historical perspective and in its current form. Next, it will examine the trajectory of mobile phone adoption and integration. Then, from the lens of information design, the chapter will investigate the issues of user-experience and mobile technology. Finally, this study will position QR codes as one solution to digital divide issues, or at least as a tool for changing the experience of disengaged community members in an increasingly digital world.

The Digital Divide

The digital divide is a relatively new term introduced by the National Telecommunications and Information Administration (NTIA) of the United States Department of Commerce (USDC) in a series of four in-depth reports released from 1995-2000. The concept of a "digital divide" separates people as either information "haves" or "have-nots" (NTIA, 1999). In the context of the 1999 NTIA report, information "haves" are individuals with Internet access at home. On the contrary, information "have-nots" include the segment of the population that lacks access to the Internet at home.

In the sobering 1998 NTIA report which further explores the digital divide, "Falling Through the Net: Defining the Digital Divide," the agency stressed that the unequal access to information is one of America's leading economic and civil rights issues. The report found minorities, the poor and the less educated were less connected to the Internet than their counterparts (NTIA, 1998). The gap in Internet access at the time left a large segment of the U.S. population without the tools necessary for full participation in an increasingly digital economy and society.

In the last decade, many organizations have worked to seek solutions to the digital divide. One notable example of the investment in the fight to bring digital inclusion is the Alliance for Digital Equality (ADE). The ADE is a non-profit advocacy organization dedicated to ensuring equal access to new broadband technologies in underserved communities. ADE brings together policy makers, thought leaders, and the media for "Digital Empowerment Summits" across the country to raise awareness about the digital divide and create solutions for bridging the widening Internet gap in America. Furthermore, ADE also donates computers to public centers for those who do not have Internet access at home. The group understands that the lack of access limits the "have-nots" from many opportunities including civic engagement, education and job growth.

The digital divide is also an issue surrounding the role of communication in America and American entitlements to telecommunication infrastructure. Under the U.S. telecommunications policy, the "universal service" directive ensures every American has access to communication services including the Internet (NTIA, 1998). The main goal of "universal service," as mandated by the Telecommunications Act of 1996, centers around open competition between communication providers (i.e. cable companies, cell phone providers). Such competition would result in affordable rates that could increase Internet usage in the electronic information age (Barshefksy, 2001). The measure seeks to ensure the "information disadvantaged" have equal access to new communication technologies to close the digital divide.

In 2003, technology report discovered over a quarter of Internet users had gone offline for an extended period of time for a number of reasons including finances and geographic location (Rainie, Madden, Boyce, Lenhart, Horrigan, Allen & O'Grady, 2003). As an example, Rainie et al. (2003) noted that disabled Americans were poorer than the general population and could not afford to pay for a high speed internet connection. These findings support the 1998 NITA survey which revealed that Internet access varied from person to person based on several factors including income, race, education, age and other demographic identifiers.

Twelve years later, in 2010, nearly all wealthy U.S. households logged onto the Internet at home, but just over half of the poorest households accessed the Internet in the same manner (Jansen, 2010). The Internet can be accessed on computers and cell phones using dial-up, broadband, or wireless networks in various places including homes, workplaces, libraries, schools, and businesses. Yet, at the same time that communities experience ubiquitous access to the Internet, each individual experiences different levels of Internet access.

In 2011, Political blogger DeVan Hankerson sounded off about the digital divide's impact on the current U.S. economy in an article titled "The Digital Divide: How The Math Works" for Politics365.com. Hankerson cites a study from the McKinsey Global Institute which found the Internet economy is responsible for 15% of the country's economic growth. Hankerson argues that full online participation is needed in the U.S. to jump start its global competitiveness. In the future, the country may suffer from allowing millions to be left behind in this digital era, when Internet dependence is growing for businesses and these same business need digitally literate workers.

Meanwhile, the Economics and Statistics Administration (ESA) and the NTIA (2011) made the case on a blog post backed by report findings that the digital divide remains a problem that cannot be solved with one silver bullet. Both government agencies recognized that multiple solutions are required to close the digital divide, including education, public computer centers, and widespread Internet access in underserved communities.

Further research suggests the question of "access" is more than the classic economic analysis of income disparity. The gap between information "rich" and the information "poor" is also a matter of race, education, and age, and location. Whites, the college-educated and the young (relatively) are more likely to have Internet access than any other group of people throughout the nation (Lenhart, 2000). In rural areas, nearly 1 and 10 Americans are without broadband access at all (White, 2012). Collectively, these findings will help advocates close the digital divide by outlining the susceptible segments of society living in underserved communities that desperately need online access.

Meanwhile, a new digital divide is emerging in our society. A 2010 Pew poll found more minorities than whites accessed the Internet using mobile technology (Washington, 2010). Mobile phones have given users inexpensive access to the World Wide Web. However, despite more people carrying portable computers in their pockets, the digital divide remains intact.

Smart phone Internet access cannot yet replace a wired high-speed Internet connection because functions such as filling out a job application or taking online classes can often only be done on a computer (Crawford, 2011). The cell phone's limited capability to provide the type of aforemetioned information is not to be blamed on the design of the device. The blame lies in the lack of ability to transmit online information through multiple devices and media. Before turning to this issue of design, this chapter will address the current state of mobile phone adoption.

Mobile Phone Adoption

Mobile phones have changed the way we communicate allowing users to stay "connected" to the information superhighway. In 2010, over 80 percent of adults in the US own a cell phone device with nearly half accessing the Internet from same tool. (Smith, 2010). The mobile phone, which is sold at a relatively low price compared to computers, has emerged as the preeminent tool for wireless Internet connection (Anderson & Rainie, 2008).

The first portable phone entered the technology scene in 1983 with the Motorola DynaTAC 8000X (The Editors, 2011). Early adopters were primarily in the business market due to the extremely high prices of the cell phone and it was mainly mounted in cars (Giachetti & Marchi, 2010). The cell phone became portable in the early 1990s. Subsequently, in the late 1990s, the cell phone became even smaller and lighter with expanded network coverage and cheaper prices for mass adoption (Giachetti & March, 2010). Since its debut, the mobile phone has penetrated the worldwide marketplace allowing individuals the ability to not only place telephone calls, but also to search for online information.

Mobile phones that offer more capabilities to communicate are referred to as smart phones. These phones allow users more options to stay connected through downloading applications, accessing Wi-Fi (wireless internet), viewing texts, sharing photos, and watching videos (Smith, 2011). Smart phones allow their users to engage in the Internet in a way unlike any other phones in history.

A 2011 report by the Pew Research Center's Internet & American Life Project suggests that one-quarter of smart phone users regularly use their cell phone to go online despite having other options for accessing the Internet. Smart phone usage for browsing the Internet is even higher for the less educated and the poor (Smith, 2011). The same study revealed that smartphone users are more likely to be non-white, college educated and in their mid-twenties. In 2010, digital strategist Susannah Fox found that 82% percent of adults have a cell phone and 6 out of 10 adults go online wirelessly with a laptop or mobile device (Fox, 2010). Future predictions peg the mobile phone as the number one connection tool worldwide by the year 2020 (Anderson & Rainie 2008).

In light of the issues raised earlier about the capability of smart phones to display online information, this chapter now turns to information design to seek solutions for using this technology to bridge the digital divide.

Information Design and the Need for Mobile Optimization

Information design is integral to a mobile phone user's response and handling of the device. Several definitions of information design inform this chapter's understanding of the field:

- Carliner (2000) defines information design as a process for preparing communication products for its intended users through analysis, planning, goal-setting, and evaluation. The strength of Carliner's definition lies in the recognition that design of information is task-oriented and user-focused.
- Mazur (2008) explores the history of information design and contributes to the conversation by suggesting information design is a

- transformative process which is vulnerable to new technologies. Mazur suggests the essence of information design will change as new ideas and practices enter the field.
- Redish (2000) introduces a dual definition for information design which focuses on the process and the presentation of information. Redish believes information designers need to understand that the creation process and the placement of information from the layout, typography, color, words and pictures are essential for user consumption of a particular communication product.
- Shedroff (2009) develops an even more user-focused definition of information design. He describes design as a process of understanding which moves from data to information to knowledge to wisdom. The importance in the transformation lies in the user's ability to comprehend new media experiences. For example, the data found on a mobile phone contains categories of user information. Through the use of the phone, the user can extract the information he or she needs, which builds knowledge. When one reflects on the personal use or uses of knowledge to share information as a digitally literate creator, then perhaps that person demonstrates wisdom.
- Shedroff (2009) also characterized information design as user-experience. Each communication product tells a unique story to its users. In some instances, the story can be misinterpreted or ignored based on the structure, context, and presentation of the information. Therefore, information might be created with the user in mind to encourage users to become producers of their own interactive experiences.

The mobile phone has design limitations. The portable nature of the device automatically brings difficulties for users. In a 2011 survey of mobile phone users, 16% of respondents reported problems viewing text, video, or photos on the small screen (Smith, 2011). In the same study, another 10% expressed difficulty entering a lot of text on their phone. These are issues of (1) the use of the device itself and (2) the presentation of information to be accessed on the smart phone.

As use of mobile phones increases with a growing reliance on the devices for Internet access, mobile optimization might be the information design answer to compensate for small screens and viewing issues. The term mobile optimization refers to the creation of a mobile-friendly version of any website which contains readable text and clickable links. With increased reliance on mobile devices for Internet connection, web designers must convert and create more web sites that are accessible across multiple platforms.

Mobile optimization would enhance the user's experience of a website and create compatibility between the device and the information viewed on it. It allows the data presented on the phone to sync with the design of the device, promoting a successful transfer of information. But while mobile optimization helps users see information once they've found it, it does not help users find information they need.

QR Code

Two dimensional bar codes (also known as quick response (QR) codes) can provide organizations with another tool to reach the public in addition to mobile optimization. This new technology can help bridge the digital divide using mobile phones that are already in the hands of most American demographics. This section will focus on the history and development of the QR code.

The QR code was created by a Japanese automotive company to track car parts in the manufacturing process in the 1990s. (Xue & Hairong, 2008). The QR code looks like a product bar code found on packaging for many retail items. Unlike, the standard bar code which contains information about a product and its price, the QR code is a visual hyperlink that can be accessed from anywhere on a mobile device. The QR code can hold a range of digital formats, such as links to text, images, audio, video and web sites (Simmon, 2010).

Any individual can create a QR code at no cost using various programs that can be found on the Internet. (Some of the available sites at the time this chapter was written include QRifier.com and uQR.me). A creator has the ability to manipulate the color, size and shape of a QR code. Also, the QR code allows creators to develop any kind of data for sharing at a higher rate.

To access the information in a QR code on a mobile phone device, a smart phone user can download a (typically free) QR code reader. Then the user uses the camera on the phone to scan the QR code and open a web browser to view the information contained in the code (Rosenbloom, 2011).

The QR code has its roots in hypertext due to its linking nature. Hypertext describes the text displayed on electronic devices that contains a link to another page elsewhere on the Internet. A user who clicks on the hypertext would be re-directed to the link page. Although, the breadth of knowledge housed on the World Wide Web may be seem daunting to cypher through, hypertext gives one the freedom to browse at will based on their own personal interests (Havice, 2002). Hypertexts are also organized in a non-linear manner. Some technology experts have deemed the QR code a "print based hypertext link".

The QR code is the next evolution in linking systems. The QR code may not look like hypertext but it serves the same, non-linear function. Furthermore, QR codes can contain links which send users directly to a web page, social networking site, Pay pal account, graphic, audio, or video element. Also, the QR code can be stored on a cell phone which makes it easier to use with repeated accesses or to share and send. The ability of QR codes to contribute to mobile optimization can increase the data information, knowledge, and wisdom of citizens on important topics that encourage civic engagement.

Concluding thoughts

As previously addressed in this chapter, fewer households have broadband Internet at home and many public libraries are struggling to secure resources to upgrade computer software and Internet connections (Kinney, 2010). Therefore, mobile phones are a vital tool for connection despite the limitations of the mobile accessible.

In today's digital age, mobile adoption is creating opportunities for greater access and participation and stands poised to be a leading contributor to bridge the digital divide in certain populations. However, the lack of websites optimized for mobile technology blocks information from the poor, the old, the less-educated and some key minority populations who rely heavily on mobile technology for Internet access. For these communities, the digital divide may actually be continuing to grow.

Hindering "cell-phone-only" users from accessing all online information creates barriers for engagement and empowerment on a daily basis. Washington writes, "It's tough to fill out a job application on a cell phone..." (2011). One would have to agree with the statement because more information is often available by logging online using a laptop or a desktop at work, home or school when compared to a smart phone.

Campbell and Kwak (2010) researched the correlation between cell phone usage and civic engagement. Their research findings indicated that competent cell phone users were more likely to be active citizens. The researchers also discovered the mobile phone's ease of use led to more individuals sharing content, more specifically political information. In addition, the relatively affordable price of cell phones increases the number of cell phone users which in turn increases the sharing content rate. Campbell and Kwak did not address the use of QR codes, but it is another tool which makes it easier to share information.

Moreover, the abilities to connect, comprehend, consume and create information across various new media platforms is an issue of digital literacy. The introduction of this book describes the skills and concepts surrounding literacy in the digital age. The QR code is a tool which can bring digital inclusion to mainstream society. The QR code gives the "digitally disenfranchised" the ability to access information, which is the first step in the quest for literacy and community engagement.

References

Anderson, J. & Rainie, L. (2008). The Future of the Internet III. Pew Internet & American Life Project. Retrieved November 2011, from http://www.pewinternet.org/Reports/2008/The-Future-of-the-Internet-II

Barshefsky, C. (2001). Trade policy for a networked world. *Foreign Affairs, 80*(2), 134-146.

Brumberger, E. (2004). The rhetoric of typography: the persona of typeface and text. *Technical Communication, 50*(2). 206.

Campbell, S. W., & Kwak, N. (2010). Mobile communication and civic life: linking patterns of use to civic and political engagement. *Journal of Communication, 60*(3).

Carliner, S. (2000). Physical, cognitive, and affective: a three-part framework for information design. *Technical Communication, 47*(4), 561-576.

Digital Divide Persists, Berkeley Study Shows. (2011). *Communications of the ACM, 54*(8), 20.

Fox, S. (2010). The power of mobile. Pew Internet & American Life Project. Retrieved from http://www.pewinternet.org/Commentary/2010/September/The-Power-of-Mobile.aspx

Giachetti, C. & Marchi, G,. (2010). Evolution of firms' product strategy over the life cycle of technology-based industries: a case study of the global mobile phone industry, 1980-2009. *Business History, 52* (7), 1123-1150.

Gilbert, M. (2010). Theorizing digital and urban inequalities. *Information, Communication & Society, 13* (7), 1000-1018.

Hankerson, D. (2011). The digial divide: how the math works. Retrieved December 2011, from http://politic365.com/2011/12/06/the-digital-divide-how-the-math-works/

Havice, B. (2002). Hypertext: a brief history. *Visual Communications Journal.* Retrieved from www.igae.org

Jansen, J. (2010). Use of the internet in higher income households. Pew Internet & American Life Project. Retrieved November 2011, from http://www.pewinternet.org/Reports/2010/Better-off-households.aspx

Jefferson, G. (2011, Mar 30). More companies shrink sites. *USA Today.*

Kinney, B. (2010). The internet, public libraries, and the digital divide. *Public Library Quarterly, 29* (2), 104-161.

Kynell, T. (2000). Readings in information/visualization/information design/information architects (book review). *Technical Communication, 9*(3), 347.

Lenhard, A. (2000). Who's Not Online. Pew Internet & American Life Project. Retrieved November 2011, from http://www.pewinternet.org/Reports/2000/Whos-Not-Online/Report/Part-1.aspx

Mazur, B. (2008). Information design in motion. In Albers M.J. (Eds.), *Content and complexity: information design in technical communication.* (pp 1-38). Mahwah, NJ: Lawrence Erlbaum Associates, Inc.

Miller, K. (2011). Conquering the digital divide. *American Libraries, 42*(7/8), 58.

National Telecommunications and Information Administration. (1995, July). Falling through the net: A survey of "have-nots" in rural and urban America. Retrieved December 2011, from http://www.ntia.doc.gov/ntiahome/fallingthru.html

National Telecommunications and Information Administration. (1998, July). Falling through the net II: new data on the digital divide. Retrieved

December 2011, from http://www.ntia.doc.gov/report/1998/falling-through-net-ii-new-data-digital-divide

National Telecommunications and Information Administration. (1999, July). Falling through the net: defining the digital divide. Retrieved December 2011, from http://www.ntia.doc.gov/legacy/ntiahome/fttn99/introduction.html

National Telecommunications and Information Administration. (2011). Broadband internet adoption moves forward, but digital divides still persists. Retrieved from http://www.ntia.doc.gov/blog/2011/broadband-internet-adoption-moves-forward-digital-divide-still-persists

Penny, J.(2011). QR codes give signage extra punch. *Buildings, 105*(9), 26.

Rainie, L., Madden, M., Boyce, A., Lenhart, A,. Horrigan J., Allen, K., & O'Grady, E. (2003). The ever-shifting internet population: a new look at internet access and the digital divide. Pew Internet & American Life Project. Retrieved December 2011, from http://www.pewinternet.org/Reports/2003/The-EverShifting-Internet-Population-A-new-look-at-Internet-access-and-the-digital-divide/06-A-new-understanding-of-internet-use/04-Intermittent-Users.aspx

Redish, J. (2000). What is information design? *Technical Communication, 47* (2), 163.

Rosenbloom, S. (2011, September 22). Want more information? Just scan me. *New York Times*. 1.

Shedroff, N. (2009). *Experience design 1.1*. (2nd ed.). San Franciso, CA: Experience Design Books.

Simmons, L. C. (2010). Smart scanning: QR Codes offer PR pros new options to connect. *Public Relations Tactics, 17*, 11.

Smith, A. (2011). Americans and their cell phones. Pew Internet & American Life Project. Retrieved from http://www.pewinternet.org/Reports/2010/Better-off-households.aspx

Smith, A. (2011a). Smartphone Adoption and Usage. Pew Internet & American Life Project. Retrieved from http://www.pewinternet.org/Reports/2011/Smartphones.aspx

The, E. (2011). 101 gadgets that changed the world. *Popular Mechanics, 188*(7), 50-68.

Trend Data (2011). Pew Internet & American Life Project. Retrieved December 2011, from http://www.pewinternet.org/Trend-Data/Internet-Adoption.aspx

Xue, D., & Hairong, L. (2008). Creative uses of QR codes in consumer communication. *International Journal of Mobile Marketing, 3*(2), 61-67.

Washington, J. (2011, January 10). For minorities, new 'digital divide' seen. *USA Today.* Retrieved December 2011, from http://www.usatoday.com/tech/news/2011-01-10-minorities-online_N.htm

White, C. (2012, February, 05). Digital divide: if you're reading this, you're one of the lucky ones [infographic]. Retrieved February 2012, from http://mashable.com/2012/02/05/digital-divide-infographic/

About the Author

Davida Jackson is the founder of Called2Connect, a digital marketing consultant agency in Charlotte, NC. She currently serves as a television news producer, a freelance reporter and an adjunct instructor at the Carolina School of Broadcasting. She is a student in the Master of Arts in Communication Program in the James L. Knight School of Communication at Queens University of Charlotte.

Investing in Digital Senior Citizens

Sandra Saburn

Mary Jo, a 71-year-old woman, typically uses a computer and high-speed Internet connection in her home when her grandchildren are there to assist her. If she wants to look something up online, she writes a note and places it beside the computer for the next time her children or grandchildren come to visit. She isn't comfortable searching by herself because she is afraid she'll break something. Mary Jo knows about the vast information online that she would like to access, but her limited training on computers leaves her afraid of them.

Louis is a 77-year-old man who worked as an electrician for more than 40 years and saved well throughout his life to fund his retirement. He enjoys keeping up with the stock market and monitoring his investments. He knows there is a great deal of information online that he would find both interesting and beneficial, but he relies on the printed resources at his local library for information. He certainly has the financial means to purchase a computer and pay for an Internet connection, but doesn't have anyone who could help him get started.

Kathy is a 74-year-old woman who uses the computer to keep in touch with her children and grandchildren in three different states. She loves sending and receiving email because it helps her stay connected with what's going on in her family. Recently, with the help of her 13 year-old granddaughter, she set up a Facebook account. On Facebook, she enjoys reading about the kids' activities, but never posts anything on the site. She occasionally uses Google to search for information and is aware that she could do much more with the computer, but isn't willing to venture out on her own to explore.

***

These examples are but three stories of the intersection of older Americans and technology. This chapter will look at the impact of technology on the lives of seniors and examine the so-called "digital divide," a term used to describe the gap between those with access to technology and those without that same access. Next, it will examine how information design can inform the conversation around seniors and technology adoption. Finally, the chapter will explore a few examples of programs that are working to span the digital divide for seniors by improving access to technology, as well as enhancing comfort using computers and their associated applications.

The Digital Divide

Wilson, Wallin, and Reiser (2003) define the digital divide as "the concept developed to describe the gap between those who are reaping the advantages of this new technology and those who are not" (p. 133). Jackson, Zhao, Kolenic, Fitzgerald, Harond and Von Eye (2008) take the definition a bit further: "Today, digital divide has new meaning. It refers to the gap in the intensity and nature of IT [information technology] use rather than the gap in access to it" (p. 437). For many, the abundance of technology and access to it is no longer the only issue, but now the divide includes inability to use the tools and discomfort associated with interpreting them.

As time progresses the digital divide encompasses the quality of the information we have access to, not just the quantity or the technical skills to find it.

> During the first decade of this century, the digital divide could be seen as an information divide (both in use and creation), and the importance of 'critical digital literacy' would become prominent. ... We were clearly becoming more concerned about what information we access, who provides it, and whether we simply consume this information uncritically or take a little effort to add to it in a meaningful way. (Modarres, 2011, p. 5)

As the information and technology available becomes more complex, the problem becomes more complex. Basic use of Internet technology is no longer a matter of finding the answer to a question; it also requires an ability to determine the validity of information. Often, this means takes sifting through much information to get to what seems to be a reasonable answer. For those new to the digital experience, this process can be overwhelming. This process is a fundamental issue of digital literacy.

Digital Literacy

If you ask 20 people for their definition of "digital literacy" you will likely get 20 different answers. But, you will probably hear some of the same words used in many – if not all – of the responses. Phrases like "technology", "computers", and "information" are often mentioned. Today's technology is so complex that it is difficult to find a definition that is universal and also detailed. United Nations Educational, Scientific and Cultural Organization (UNESCO) is concerned about literacy on a global scale. Initially they considered digital literacy "as the set of technical skills – reading, writing, and calculating" (Meneses & Momino, 2010, p. 199). Ultimately the organization found it was "necessary to expand its definition to refer to a multidimensional and complex process that is situated and shaped – in a dynamic fashion nonetheless – by culture, language and socioeconomic conditions" (p. 199).

UNESCO's expansion of the definition looks like this: "The acquisition and development of literacy are therefore not simply the achievement of a neutral and decontextualized cognitive ability to read and write. On the contrary, it is the development of the history-, culture-, and context-dependent abilities to master the informational and communicational process in social practice" (p. 199).

In The Information Society (2008), Hassan argues that "information has become the central organizing force of society and that this change may be the most significant societal shift since the Industrial Revolution" (p. 23). He believes speed or timeliness is the most important aspect of today's information technology. It is no longer enough to come up with the right answer, but you must come up with it quickly.

When Renee Hobbs investigated digital media literacy in the Aspen Institute's *Digital & Media Literacy: A Plan of Action*, she identified five core competencies of such literacy: access, analysis, creation, reflection, and action. As this chapter has already mentioned, the core issues facing our senior citizens seem to revolve first around access and analysis. This generalization is not meant capture the experience of all members of this group, but advances the notion that digital literacy is an issue for all in our population, including seniors.

Senior Citizens

In the United States, senior citizens are defined by the US Census Bureau as those aged 65 and older. According to the results from the 2010 U.S. Census, more people fell into the category "age 65 and older" in 2010 than on any previous census. From a generational perspective, people aged 65 and older can be grouped into three generations: Baby Boomers, the Silent Generation, and The Greatest Generation.

Baby Boomers are defined as those individuals born between 1946 and 1964 (U.S. Census Bureau). The first of the Baby Boomers turned 65 on January 1, 2011. While not currently the largest section of the senior citizen population in the U.S., they are expected to quickly fill that role. By the time the youngest Baby Boomer turns 65, the U.S. Census Bureau estimates that senior citizens will represent 19.7% of the population – a rise from 7.3% in 2000 (U.S. Census Bureau, 2010). That means there will be more than 71 million senior citizens in the U.S., and many of them will be Baby Boomers.

Those born between 1925 and 1946 are referred to as the Silent Generation (Time, 1951). This term was coined by Time magazine in their cover story on the generation coming of age in 1951. The Great Depression and World War II marked the early experiences of this generation, and many of them served in or were affected by the Korean War.

The oldest segment of today's senior citizen population is from the Greatest Generation, born between 1901 and 1924. Journalist Tom Brokaw, used this term to describe this group of individuals that he believed comprised, "the greatest generation any society has ever produced" (1998, p. xxxviii). According to the 2010 U.S. Census, there are still more than 4 million members of this generation living in the U.S.

How Seniors Interact with the Digital World

The Pew Research Center's Internet & American Life Project (2009) reported that Internet use still varies significantly across age groups. While 87% of teens 12–17 and 82% of 18–24 year-olds are now online, only 57% of adults between the ages of 65 and 69 report using the Internet, and the numbers drop dramatically after age 70 (26%) and 76 (17%) (Jung et al., 2010, p. 194).

Likewise, use of other technology-related products is reduced among seniors. A survey conducted by The Pew Research Center's Internet & American Life Project (2010), 48% of adults ages 66 to 74 and only 28% of seniors 75 and older, owned a desktop computer (Pew, 2010). Ownership of a laptop computer was even lower: 30% and 10% respectively. Without ownership of one of these devices, access to the Internet is greatly reduced.

According to research conducted by Lam and Lee in Hong Kong, senior citizens (that country considers senior citizens to be 55 or older) were less likely than other demographics to use the Internet – even in homes where a computer was available. Despite not frequently using the technology, seniors did want to use computers. Lam and Lee (2006) cited the following reasons for this desire reported by seniors: (1) to acquire new knowledge; (2) to read news through online newspaper or listen to online radio; (3) to keep up with the trend in surfing the information superhighway; (4) to keep in contact with distant relatives and friends through e-mail; and (5) to broaden discussion topics with my family, friends, and the younger generation. (Lam & Lee, 2006, p. 201).

So, even though seniors reported using the technology less than other demographics, their desire to use the technology remained high. This gap in desire versus use requires us to question the variables that lead to access barriers for seniors. One framework for assessing this gap is the lens of information design.

Information Design

In *Content and Complexity*, Michael Albers and Beth Mazur identify 6 definitions from various experts in the information design field (2003, pp. 2-4). For its simplicity, this chapter will work with the included definition put forth by the Information Design Journal: "Information design is the art and the science of presenting information so that it is understandable and easy to use: effective, efficient and attractive" (Albers & Mazur, 2003, p. 3). Many design characteristics might be equally "attractive" (or unattractive) to senior citizens and young adults. But when it comes to being "effective" and "efficient," seniors may likely have different requirements than younger generations.

In the introduction to the book, Albers & Mazur also state, "to the user, the information content is the system. Unless that information is properly designed, displayed, and can be manipulated for interpretation, the information (and consequently, the system) is a failure" (2003, p. 6). Much like the saying "beauty is in the eye of the beholder," the user is the ultimate judge of the usability of a system or product.

With the cost for technology plummeting over recent years, financial considerations are not likely to be the barrier most senior citizens face in using technology. More likely their lack of technology adoption might be attributable to two factors: design of the products and lack of confidence in knowing how to use them. The first concern is an issue of information design and user experience: designers need to first be cognizant of the need to consider seniors in information and product design. The second concern may be partly alleviated by solving the design issues that make technology unfriendly to older people and could go a long way toward easing their hesitations for using it.

Effective Product Design

The usability of the products has emerged as an issue for seniors. Today's mass-market technology is designed for a one-size-fits-all audience and as a result leaves out many of the people on the extremes of society. In the case of senior citizens, that is a very large portion of the population to disregard. In *Seniors and Technology: Results from a Field Study*, McMurtrey, Zeltmann, Downey, and McGaughey (2011) state, "It surely seems that technology, from computing to cell phones, is not designed with the elderly in mind. Our research indicates that this divide may be shrinking. Perhaps it is time for designers, marketers, and researchers to examine whether this segment of the population deserves more consideration" (p. 23). Today, most technology introduced to the market (think iPads and smart phones) is believed to be intuitive to use. Walk into any Apple store and you will see very young children picking up devices and using them without any instruction at all. However, many of the people who are now seniors would never think to do that without knowing the "right" way to use it.

One of the contributing factors to the divide is that older "adults are subject to age-related declines in visual and auditory sensory processes, motor skills and cognitive abilities" (McMurtrey, p. 22). Having compromised abilities makes seniors less likely to be adventurous with what many see as expensive toys. They are afraid of damaging the items at hand or at causing some irreparable harm to the computer system.

Furthermore, "some seniors suffer from age-related debilitations, such as declining eyesight, mobility, coordination, hand-to-eye movement, etc., that physically prevent them from utilizing IT-related devices. And most digital products are not designed with seniors in mind. For instance, most technology devices employ very small plugs, wires, keyboards, interfaces, mouse, etc. that may be difficult for seniors" (McMurtrey et al, 2011, pp. 22). Many computer designers likely have never considered the effect that these small components have on senior citizens unless they have seen someone with failing eyesight or trembling hands attempt to use the product. These are easily resolved problems, but go against the current fashion of making products smaller, thinner, and more sensitive to touch. Avoiding a one-size-fits-all approach will improve the ability of seniors to use technology without having to make it unattractive to other users.

Of course, this isn't to say that all senior citizens are frail with diminishing eyesight, gnarled fingers, and significant mobility issues. But with a population that is living longer and increasing as a percentage of the total US population, the design of products for various demographics is an important design consideration. Technology designers would be doing a great service to older consumers by offering options that better fit their physical needs and make using a computer a more enjoyable experience. This would involve not only reimagining the physical design of the computer, but also the software running on it, and the types of owners' manuals and other written or digital instructions that accompany the product.

Designing with the senior end-user in mind is also very important in terms of websites. As Beth Mazur pointed out in *Content and Complexity*, "For reasons of cost and efficiency, more governments, non-profits, and corporations will be making information and services available on the Web. Assisting people with navigation tasks through multitudes of pages is certainly a worthwhile task; so is helping people make use of the information once they find it" (2009, p. 30). It isn't enough to give people the ability to find information; it has to be designed to be usable after it is discovered.

Lack of Confidence

As computers evolve and become more compact and portable, it is easy to imagine that many seniors may be hesitant to upgrade their current desktop computer for something that they perceive to be harder to use. One of the findings of Lam & Lee's research was "that the digital divide gap may be narrowed by continuously offering suitably tailored computer training programs to adults age 55 or older... Through a better understanding of this population segment, new markets may be discovered and services and products can be tailor-made to their special needs, such as online banking, user interface designs, new adaptive software and hardware, and so on" (Lam & Lee, 2006, pp. 202). This portion of information design is one of confidence and training. In this area, fortunately, much is being done to identify the needs of seniors and put programs in place that meet those needs.

Below are examples of research and programs that are designed for the senior citizen as a user of digital technologies. In Los Angeles, an expansive program was undertaken to provide free internet access and training to first-generation immigrants in their native language. Jung et. al. (2010) found that "even when they were provided with the opportunity of free enrollment and training in their native languages, only a small percentage of the seniors took advantage of this opportunity. It suggests that closing the gap of digital divide is not as easy as providing access." (p. 207). The study continues:

> To enhance the success of senior centers implementing Internet training and access programs, a strong educational and recruitment campaign to address the fear of the seniors is important. Based on our findings, we also suggest that it might be effective to tap into anxiety about aging by suggesting that there may be benefits to computer and Internet literacy that are important to healthy aging. (Jung et al., 2010, p. 207)

Rather than approaching technology training with an "everyone else knows how to do this, you should do", attitude, training will be more effective if seniors are educated about what is it in for them. What will they get out of being digitally literate? What kind of information is available and how will it improve their quality of life?

In rural California, the Community Media Access Project (CMAP) provides training and education to citizens in economically struggling areas. This project is part of a group called ZeroDivide and is one of seven programs funded by the American Recovery and Reinvestment Act of 2009. It provided nearly $5 billion to enhance the adoption of high-speed broadband internet throughout the country (McGrath, 2011, p. 24).

The Knight Community Information Challenge, funded by the John S. & James L. Knight Foundation, provided more than $14 million to 71 community and place-based foundations over the past four years. The goal of the program is improve access to technology and particularly information in underserved areas. An evaluation of the "BG Time" program highlighted the Central Carolina Community Foundation's work to train "seniors in the community to build their digital literacy skills" (Knight Foundation, 2012). The program began serving a specific region of South Carolina and was so successful it has been expanded to a statewide initiative that encourages the voices of seniors in civic dialogue.

Many other organizations across the country provide training, education and hardware to help seniors bridge the digital divide. Whether these programs are massive such as the $50 million invested by ZeroDivide (McGrath, 2011, pp. 4-5), or small programs staffed by volunteers, each has its role to play in improving access to information for seniors.

Conclusion

In less than 20 years, nearly 20% of the U.S. population will be age 65 or older. While we cannot even imagine what our technology might be like in that period of time, it is fair to say that it will be of great significance in our everyday lives. For that reason, it is imperative that we don't leave behind this large population of Americans.

To ensure this doesn't happen, we have to first take a look at the needs and desires of the senior population and identify how technology is currently being used and how it could benefit these individuals. We also must look closely at the design of both products and technology platforms to ensure that they don't take a one-size-fits-all approach that will not work for many seniors.

A suggestion for future study is to evaluate the many programs offered across the U.S. in cities and towns that are designed specifically to ensure that senior citizens don't fall victim to the digital divide. Identifying best practices from these programs and making other non-profit organizations and municipalities aware of them will be the fastest way to disseminate information and affect the greatest number of people.

Most importantly, the time to take action on these initiatives is now. As more and more Baby Boomers continue to approach the mantle of senior citizen, it means the population on one side of the digital divide is growing, while the younger generation is more capable of keeping up. The longer we wait to address this issue, the more complex the problem will be to solve.

References

Agarwal, R., Animesh, A., & Prasad, K. (2009). Social interactions and the "digital divide": Explaining variations in internet use. *Information Systems Research, 20*(2), 277-294.

Albers, M. J. & Mazur, B. (Eds.). (2003). *Context and complexity: Information design in technical communication.* New York, NY: Routledge.

Brokaw, T. (1998). *The greatest generation.* New York: Random House.

Carliner, S. (2000, Fourth quarter). Physical, cognitive, and affective: A three-part framework for information design. *Technical Communication,* 561-576.

DiMaggio, P., Hargittai, E., Neuman, W. R., & Robinson, J. P. (2001). Social implications of the internet. Annual Review of Sociology, *27*, 307-356.

Hassan, R. (2008). *The information society: Cyber dreams and digital nightmares.* Cambridge, U.K.: Polity Press.

Jackson, L. A., Zhao, Y., Kolenic, A., Fitzgerald, H. E., Harold, R., & Von Eye, A. (2008). Race, gender, and information technology use: The new digital divide. *CyberPsychology & Behavior, 11*(4), 437-442.

Jaeger, B. (2004, February). Trapped in the digital divide? Old people in the information society. *Science Studies, 17*(2), 5-22.

James, J. (2008). Digital divide complacency: Misconceptions and dangers. *The Information Society, 24,* 54-61. doi: 10.1080/01972240701774790

Jung, Y., Peng, W., Moran, M., Jin, S. A., McLaughlin, M., Cody, M., Jordan-Marsh, M., Albright, J., & Silverstein, M. (2010). Low-income minority seniors' enrollment in a cybercafé: Psychological barriers to crossing the digital divide. *Educational Gerontology, 36,* 193-212. doi: 10.1080/0361270903183313.

Knight Foundation (2012). BG Time – Central Carolina Community Foundation. Retrieved February 2012 from http://www.knightfoundation.org/grants/20082483/

Lam, J. C. Y. & Lee, M. K. O. (2006). Digital inclusiveness: Longitudinal study of internet adoption by older adults. *Journal of Management Information Systems, 22*(4), 177-206.

Mazur, B. (2009). Information design in motion. In M. Albers (Ed.), *Content and Complexity: Information Design in Technical Communication* (pp. 15-38). New York, NY: Routledge.

McGrath, M. (2011). Zeroing the Divide: Promoting broadband use and media savvy in underserved communities. *National Civic Review*, 24-28. doi: 10.1002/ncr.20068.

McMurtrey, M. E., Zeltmann, S. M., Downey, J. P., & McGaughey, R. E. (2011). Seniors and technology: Results from a field study. *Journal of Computer Information Systems*, 22-30.

Meneses, J. & Momino, J. M. (2010). Putting digital literacy in practice: How schools contribute to digital inclusion in the network society. *The Information Society*, 26, pp. 197-208.

Modarres, A. (2011, Fall). Beyond the digital divide. *National Civic Review*, 4-7. Doi: 10.1002/ncr.20069.

The Pew Internet & American Life Project. (2009). Generational differences in online activity. Retrieved December 2, 2011 from http://www.pewinternet.org/Reports/2009/Generations-Online-in-2009/Generational-Differences-in-Online-Activities.aspx

The Pew Internet & American Life Project. (2011). Generations and their gadgets: Who owns what? Retrieved March 2, 2012 from http://www.pewinternet.org/infographics/2011/generations-and-gadgets.aspx

Prensky, M. (2001). Digital natives, digital immigrants. *On the Horizon, 9*(5). NCB University Press. Retrieved from http://www.marcprensky.com/writing/Prensky%20%20Digital%20Natives,%20Digital%20Immigrants%20-%20Part1.pdf

Saunders, E. J. (2004). Maximizing computer use among the elderly in rural senior centers. *Educational Gerontology, 30*, 573-585. doi: 10.1080/03601270490466967

United States Census Bureau (2010). 2010 Census Demographic Profiles. Retrieved from http://2010.census.gov/2010census/data/

United States Census Bureau (2010). The older populations: 2010 (2010 Census briefs. Retrieved from http://www.census.gov/prod/cen2010/briefs/c2010br-09.pdf

Valadez, J. R. & Duran, R. (2007, February/March). Redefining the digital divide: Beyond access to computers and the internet. *The High School Journal*, 31-44.

Williams, S. D. (2007, October). *User experience design for technical communication: Expanding our notions of quality information design.* Paper presented at the Professional Communication Conference, Seattle, WA. Abstract retrieved from http://ieeexplore.ieee.org/xpl/freeabs_all.jsp?arnumber=4464076

Wilson, K. R., Wallin, J. S., & Reiser, C. (2003). Social stratification and the digital divide. *Social Science Computer Review, 21*, 133-143.

About the Author

Sandra Saburn is Manager for Marketing & Development at Mann Travels and recently served as a Career Management Consultant at Right Management and Owner of Coastal Resume Writers. She is a masters student in the James L. Knight School of Communication graduate programs.

Editor's note

The book originated in a graduate seminar on digital communication in the James L. Knight School of Communication at Queens University of Charlotte. The authors come from diverse backgrounds and a wide range of professional and academic experiences including marketing executives, non-profit administrators, news producers, professors, and university administrators.

We celebrate the James L. Knight School of Communication's special mission to increase digital and media literacy in Charlotte, North Carolina, an effort endowed by a grant from the John S. & James L. Knight Foundation. Part of our goal in this book is to add to the conversation surrounding digital and media literacy and its impact on communities.

We would like to thank the faculty, staff, and students in the Knight School for their overwhelming support of this book project. The graduate faculty led by Dr. Kim Weller Gregory encouraged this venture and supported the idea and the authors involved.

As part of the community of Queens University of Charlotte, the authors all value the university's motto: *non ministrare, sed ministrare* – "not to be served, but to serve." Each of these authors shares my hope that the chapters in this book will inspire all of us to think about our communities however we define them: What kinds of experiences are we providing for them? How can we strengthen our communities? And, how might digital media and information design be combined to better engage the communities we serve?

John A. McArthur, Ph.D.

Made in the USA
Lexington, KY
22 November 2015